STRANGE
NEW HAMPSHIRE
Renee Mallett

Schiffer Publishing Ltd®

4880 Lower Valley Road Atglen, Pennsylvania 19310

Designed by "Sue"
Type set in CosmicTwo/New Baskerville BT
ISBN: 978-0-7643-3475-7
Printed in The United States of America

Schiffer Books are available at special discounts for bulk purchases for sales promotions or premiums. Special editions, including personalized covers, corporate imprints, and excerpts can be created in large quantities for special needs. For more information contact the publisher:

Published by Schiffer Publishing Ltd.
4880 Lower Valley Road
Atglen, PA 19310
Phone: (610) 593-1777; Fax: (610) 593-2002
E-mail: Info@schifferbooks.com

For the largest selection of fine reference books on this and related subjects, please visit our web site at **www.schifferbooks.com**
We are always looking for people to write books on new and related subjects. If you have an idea for a book please contact us at the above address.

This book may be purchased from the publisher.
Include $5.00 for shipping.
Please try your bookstore first.
You may write for a free catalog.

In Europe, Schiffer books are distributed by
Bushwood Books
6 Marksbury Ave.
Kew Gardens
Surrey TW9 4JF England
Phone: 44 (0) 20 8392-8585; Fax: 44 (0) 20 8392-9876
E-mail: info@bushwoodbooks.co.uk
Website: www.bushwoodbooks.co.uk

DEDICATION

This book is dedicated to Gabriel,
Gwendolyn, and Penelope,
who spend more time in old cemeteries
than any of the other kids we know.

ACKNOWLEDGMENTS

Somehow or other people have gotten the mistaken impression that books are created by one person, sitting at a computer desk, armed with a cup of coffee. Not so! It takes many cups of coffee and many people to create a book. I am deeply indebted to Dinah Roseberry and the other fine folks at Schiffer Publishing who guide these creations from my head into book form.

Many other people have had their hand in helping create this book, too, from the people who have shared their stories, to book sellers, to my family, who are always there with their patience and support. So, many thanks to all of them and also to you, the reader. I get a lot of nice emails and meet a lot of nice people at book signings and lectures who have read my books. That more than anything, is what makes all the hard work (and all the jittery sleepless nights from all that coffee) worth it.

CONTENTS

Histories, Legends, and Lore

The Firemen's Riot

Nathaniel Perkins knew nothing good was going to come of holding the Firemen's Muster in the city of Manchester. As a saloon owner, he should have been thrilled at the prospect; literally thousands of firemen from all over the north east would descend on the burgeoning city for a long weekend, bringing along plenty of money for beer, girls, and gambling. As the owner of Washington House, a prominent night spot in the city, Nathaniel could expect that a good portion of those out-of-towner dollars would end up in his own pockets.

But nobody could say Perkins wasn't aware of the big picture. There were some important facts that all the other saloon owners seemed to be overlooking. Manchester was a city, growing every day, but in 1859 it was about as close to a Wild West frontier town as any city in New England could claim to be. Manchester had begun life as a company town, created, owned and operated by the Amoskeag Mills. Becoming its own city had been a learning experience. The city was still much in need of basic services towns needed to be self-sufficient, like policemen, and was high on shady connections. Manchester could boast more than its fair share of gambling halls.

But the idea of all those tourism dollars clouded the vision of too many people and, no matter how much Nathaniel Perkins tried to reason with the other business owners, the convention was welcomed to the city with more than open arms.

The highlight of the September festival was the Firemen's Muster. For the Muster a flagpole was erected in Merrimack Commons and topped with a five-foot-tall statue of a fireman. During the Muster hand pumped fire engines would surround it and one by one the companies of each fire engine would take turns to prove which could shoot a stream of water the highest distance. The first place winners would walk away with $400, a hefty sum in those days.

Needless to say, firemen poured into the Queen City for the festivities. The city swelled considerably under the pressure of 2,000 rowdy firemen (and an uncountable amount of various hangers-on looking for a good time, or their slice of the profits the good time would generate) looking for places to stay and things to do. Some residents started to complain that Manchester had turned into a shanty town. Every farmer with a field, or every home with a patch of grass, offered up the space, for a price, to anyone who wanted to build a shelter for the weekend. It was the first hint that the Firemen's Muster wasn't going to be the headache-free fun that residents had been assured of when the city decided to host the event. Tent villages sprung up, were knocked down by the careless antics of drunks, and rose back up again in the light of morning. It was a mad house by all accounts. Even so, things were running fairly smoothly, all considering, at least until the night of September 14.

Underhill's saloon and gambling house was the place to be that evening. Filled beyond capacity with tourists, the gambling reached epic proportions. A fireman by the name of Hepburn, from Charlestown, Massachusetts, had been doing pretty well at cards. Deciding he was done for the night, or at least that he was ready to move on to the next saloon down the line, he cashed in his chips. In the pile of bills the bank handed him, he found a counterfeit $5 bill—a very obvious fake. For whatever reason, he didn't immediately hand the bill back to the money man. Instead he walked back to the card table where he had been playing Faro (a popular card game at the time) all night. Hepburn handed his faked five dollars to the card dealer and asked for an equal number of chips in return.

The dealer, on the grounds that it was a counterfeit bill, refused to accept it.

Furious, and more than just a little drunk, Hepburn raised a fuss that soon attracted the attention of everyone in the saloon. The dealer was a former prize fighter. Egged on by the crowd, things quickly got out of hand. Whether the dealer took the first swing or Hepburn did is debatable, but what happened next has gone down in Manchester history.

The townies took the side of the saloon. The firemen took the side of their colleague. Everyone else took the side of whomever appeared to be winning at any given moment. In an instant, the entire gambling hall was duking it out. With fists flying, tables overturning, and broken bottles swinging, it was an all out knock 'em out brawl. In a short period of time, the gambling hall was annihilated and the crowd moved on to their next target.

Underhill's saloon was located in the basement of Elm House, so that was the next place the mob went on their path of destruction. The building was still standing come morning, but it was totally gutted inside and without a single window left intact. Out on the streets, the mob rampaged and rumors, threats, and flat-out lies began to fly around rapidly. The mob grew and grew as it went up and down Manchester's streets breaking windows and bottles, lighting fire to gambling halls, and overturning anything not firmly nailed down. Later on, after the damage was assessed, it would be estimated that the crowd dumped a good 300 gallons of liquor into the Manchester streets as they plundered every saloon and gambling hall they came across.

They trashed the infamous Roby Saloon, then one owned by Sam Perkins. Both Perkins, and Manchester mayor E. W. Harrington, called Nathaniel Perkins to tell him he had been right and to warn him that the mob was on their way to his place. Nathaniel, who had been expecting something like this from the beginning, walked outside, locked his saloons doors and waited calmly, a loaded pistol in each hand, for the crowd to arrive.

"Gentlemen, this place is closed to the public," Perkins told the mob in his quiet, refined voice when they arrived at his saloon. "I'll kill anyone who attempts to come in these doors or he'll kill me."

As if of one mind, the crowd walked away from Nathaniel Perkin's establishment without so much as throwing a single solitary stone. The rampage continued on through the night and when the morning finally came, the only saloon still standing intact in the city of Manchester was the one owned by Nathaniel Perkins. The brawling firemen had started a fire that wiped out a large portion of the city and the riot would go down as the worst in Manchester's history.

There were long ranging consequences from the fireman's riot. The city cracked down on saloons and began to raid them regularly. The city also began to employ more police. And Nathaniel Perkins? From that time until he died he was known around Manchester as Two Gun Perkins.

The flag pole remained in Merrimack Commons for several years as a reminder of the Firemen's Muster. After a time it became unsteady and was taken down. A man named Frank Hamilton got a hold of the carefully crafted fireman topper of the flagpole and set it up in his shop window. Frank could make the case that he had some small claim to the statue. While it had been sculpted by George Roberts, it was Frank's brother who was in charge of gilding the statue after it was made. Even so, the Manchester Fire Department felt that it was a point of honor that they own the sculpture.

Frank was agreeable but no fool when it came to the value of what was sitting in his store window. He agreed the firemen could take the thing — for a price. The fire department all chipped in and started saving towards the purchase.

But it wasn't meant to be. In a final piece of irony, the statue was destroyed before they could save up the asking price. It was demolished in a fire in 1870.

PIRATES

New England doesn't usually come immediately to mind when it comes to pirate hotspots, but in the years gone by, many of the most famous buccaneers of the pirate age came through this area at one point or another. New Hampshire may have only eighteen miles of coastline, the shortest of any New England state except for Vermont, but it had more than its fair share of pirates stop by. Many of them retired to the Granite State, using it as an out of the way hideout when things got to difficult for them elsewhere, or they stopped by while on their way to someplace else. It was also a place to bury treasure and leave wives. More than a few pirate folk are rumored to still be haunting the area to this day.

The Isles of Shoals, located just ten short miles away from the city of Portsmouth and New Hampshire's coast, are the center of the states pirate laden history. Originally called Smith's Isles, in honor of Captain John Smith, the name was later changed to the Isles of Shoals, in honor of the abundance of shoals of fish which flourished near the islands. Today the Isles of Shoals are shared by the states of Maine and New Hampshire. The nine islands that make up the Isles are Smuttynose Island, Appledore, Star, Seavey, Malaga, Cedar, Lunging, Duck, and White. Despite their diminutive size, they have played a big role in the history and development of both states.

THE LOST TREASURE OF
THE FLYING SCOT

Some people, it seems, are just born bad. Take Sandy Gordon. Born in Glasgow, Scotland, young Sandy Gordon proved to be so unmanageable, at such a young age, that his parents wrote him off as a ner'er-do-well and tossed him out on the streets while he was still just a young man. Gordon bummed around Glasgow for awhile before being hired as a crew member on a merchant ship called *The Porpoise*. This could have been an opportunity for the seventeen-year-old Gordon to turn his life around, but instead, he chaffed under the menial chores he was given, talked back as much as possible, and made designs on the Captain's impressionable young daughter who was along for the trip.

The Captain could put up with a lot but, as everyone knows, you don't mess around with your bosses' daughter and expect to get by unscathed. Gordon was whipped, severely, and locked in the ships hold for a lengthy period of time. But don't think that being punished did anything to discourage Sandy Gordon. As soon as his incarceration was up, Gordon found some like-minded scoundrels onboard and they mutinied. It took Sandy Gordon only three days to take over the ship.

Once in charge, the sociopathic Gordon stripped the former Captain naked, whipped him over a hundred times, and then burned his eyes out with hot pokers. As if that wasn't enough, he then threw the man overboard to a watery death. *The Porpoise* was now under the command of a very dangerous man.

Gordon talked the crew into becoming pirates and their cruelties were renowned throughout the British Isles and the rest of Europe. The crew of *The Porpoise* was legendary for its violence and for their unrelenting raids against villages. In time, they amassed a fortune. But the crew came to be as unhappy under Gordon as they were under the merchant they'd originally set sail with. Gordon was hoarding millions in gold and silver, all while working them to the bone and paying them only a bare pittance. He was as brutish with his own men as he was with the innocent villagers they pillaged. Eventually, they decided they'd had enough of him.

In the end, the crew of *The Porpoise* were not as pitiless with Sandy Gordon as he had been with his own Captain. When the crew took control of the ship, they didn't torture Gordon and they didn't throw him overboard. Instead, he was placed aboard a rowboat with a meager store of supplies and left at sea. For most men, this would have been a death sentence, but Gordon was a survivor and it would take more than that to take the bloodthirsty pirate down.

As luck would have it, Gordon would soon wash up along the shores of a small island. Luckier still, the island had a source of fresh water, an abandoned farmhouse, and some fields left over from the farmers day that had gone wild and flourished. With his basic needs taken care of, all Sandy had to do was sit and wait. He had food, water, and nothing but time.

In 1712, a ship approached the island. A rowboat full of men came ashore asking for fresh water, which Sandy had in abundance. While the men filled whatever was handy with water to bring back to their ship, they got to talking with the castaway. Somehow in the course of conversation it became clear that the Captain of the ship they arrived on was none other than Edward Treach himself. Treach, of course, is more infamous under his professional name, Blackbeard the Pirate.

Luck, it seemed, was more than just a little on Sandy Gordon's side.

He talked his way onto Blackbeard's ship for a meeting with the renowned pirate and then he managed to talk his way into a place on the ship's crew. To be fair, Gordon did have some experience as a pirate. He did well under Blackbeard. Or else Blackbeard was mindful of the fact that Gordon also had some experience carrying off a successful mutiny. He soon helped Gordon get his own pirate ship, christened *The Flying Scot*.

Time had not mellowed Gordon. He was as fearsome a pirate as any that had ever sailed the seven seas. While most pirates seemed to be in it for the money, Gordon was in it as much for the sadism as for the gold. But the gold was a powerful motivator as well. In the few years he manned *The Flying Scot,* Gordon quickly regained his lost fortune and then some. Eventually, he decided to go to the Americas, a pirate haven at the time, and became semi-retired.

Gordon made a home for himself on White Island, off the coast of New Hampshire. He'd rest a few months at his home and then, feeling the urge for adventure, would take off for a bit on his ship. Every time he came back he buried another chest full of gold and silver somewhere near his home. Mentally he declined rapidly, becoming more and more paranoid, hoarding more and more gold from his crew. In time, he might have ended up the way he did before, with an angry crew shoving him off to sea for his avarice, but instead, a much worse foe came ashore.

Sandy received word that a British Man 'O War ship was spotted on its way to White Island. It is unclear if the ship knew Gordon had made a home there and were on their way to retrieve him or if Gordon's increasingly paranoid mind just decided they were. Either way he was sure the jig was up. He pulled up as many chests full of riches he could and lugged them aboard *The Flying Scot.* He was just about to make a fast getaway when he saw the British ship looming on the horizon.

The battle between the ships reached epic proportions. Cannons blasted away, filling the air with burning smoke. Eventually, it became clear that this was a fight that Sandy Gordon could not win. Realizing he was about to be taken prisoner and hanged for the crime of piracy, Gordon grabbed a torch and rushed into the ships powder room. He was determined not to be taken alive.

The powder caught, and in an instant, the ship, its crew and Sandy Gordon were obliterated. When the smoke cleared all the

British had was a few splinters of wood bobbing in the cold blue waters of the Atlantic. Also gone, sunk to the bottom of the sea where it remains to this day, is whatever gold Gordon managed to lug onto *The Flying Scot* before attempting his getaway. It has been estimated to be a fortune worth several million dollars.

BLACKBEARD

Not much is known for sure about the young Blackbeard. He was born in Bristol, England, sometime in the late 1600s and his given name was Edward Treach, or Teach, or Thatch. For that matter, his first name may not have been Edward; it could have been Edwin. Some sources have given him the name Edward Drummond. On top of not being 100% sure of his name, we also don't really know how he ended up at sea. He may, or may not, have served in the British navy in the War of Spanish Succession. He might have been the son of a pirate to begin with. Just about the only thing we do know for sure is that at some point he became a pirate and people started to call him Blackbeard.

His first known job as a pirate was as a crew member under the pirate Captain Benjamin Hornigold. Blackbeard would become a pirate captain in his own right when Hornigold was overthrown by his crew and Blackbeard was elected to serve as Captain in his place. Blackbeard gladly took command of Hornigold's fleet and promptly armed the best ship out of the lot with a staggering amount of firepower and renamed the vessel *Queen Anne's Revenge*. It would remain his favorite ship for all of his pirating career.

There is a great deal of myth that has been built up about Treach, and much of it was purposely cultivated by the great pirate himself. Blackbeard never allowed himself to be seen without his feathered recorder hat, quite fashionable in a time when pirates went for a more low-key look. He was always armed for any eventuality, making sure to always have a vast array of swords, knives, and pistols on his person. He braided matches into his beard and he would light these on fire on fire during battles, creating a dark cloud of smoke billowing around his terrifying face. During Blackbeard's lifetime, there were many who claimed the man was Satan himself. Blackbeard has been accused of everything from periodically killing his crew to keep future crews in line, to watching as the crew took intimate liberties his wife. The truth is that Blackbeard was one of the most humane and employee-friendly pirates to have ever sailed the seven seas. Most likely, Blackbeard never killed anyone himself and relied solely on his reputation to persuade people. Blackbeard is known to have run a tight ship; he followed pirate laws to the letter, and offered his crew mates a type of disability and life insurance. A pirate that was injured while fighting alongside Blackbeard would be taken care of for the rest of his life. If a pirate died while in Blackbeard's employ, he did so knowing that a cash settlement would reach his family.

In the end, there are two things that Blackbeard has remained most known for, the first of which is his many wives. Although facts about Blackbeard are sketchy at best and as a pirate, Blackbeard didn't bother with such niceties as church weddings, the pirate is said to have married as many as fourteen women. The only story that overshadows his overzealous matrimonial leanings is the one about his vast treasure. It has long been rumored that Blackbeard had acquired a treasure unmatched by that of any other buccaneer and that he buried this treasure . . . well, somewhere. You'll find rumors of Blackbeard's treasure being buried everywhere from Jamaica, to the Carolinas, to, of course, the Isles of Shoals off the coast of New Hampshire. No matter how often historians point out the unlikelihood that Blackbeard's stolen booty ever amounted to anything more then the $2,500 he got when he sold his ship upon retirement, and that there is even less evidence that Blackbeard ever buried any of his earnings, the stories have gained too much strength over the years to be so easily forgotten.

That Blackbeard's ghost has been reported by witnesses on just about every island in the Isles of Shoals only adds credence (in some circles) to the idea that his treasure can be found there. While witnesses can't seem to decide which island he haunts, they are all in agreement that he appears dressed in the height of 1700s pirate fashion, with a wild look in his eyes, and that, by his actions, he is clearly searching desperately for something. Could that something be the fabulous, and most likely entirely mythical, pirate treasure he hid here so long ago? Or could it be one of his fourteen unlucky wives he is looking for?

As little is known about Blackbeard, even less is known about his wives, other than that they had a terrible taste in husbands. One was said to have been abandoned by the pirate on the Isles of Shoals when a British war ship was seen approaching the islands. Treach implored his wife, only a teenager, to stay on the island and warn off anyone who came looking for the treasure. Just before he left, he made her vow she'd remain faithful to him and his treasure, until Doomsday if need be. Foolishly the young girl agreed.

Nothing is known of the life the girl made for herself in New Hampshire or how she eventually died, but much is known of the wife's afterlife. To this day she is sometimes seen crying, walking the beach agitatedly in a long green velvet cloak, with a jumble of sea-blown blond hair blowing out behind her. She stands on the rocks overlooking the sea expectantly, and can sometimes be heard softly whispering "He will return."

Again, it would seem that treasure hunters would only have to follow the ghost of Blackbeard's wife and they'd find the location of his treasure, since she was left behind to oversee it. But Blackbeard's wife has been reported by witnesses on nearly as many islands as he has!

APPLEDORE ISLAND

If no one is sure which island Blackbeard and his wife are haunting, everyone knows where to find the fearsome specter of Philip Babb. In life, Babb was constable on Appledore Island . . . an interesting career path for a man who was once numbered among the crew of Captain Kidd.

Captain Kidd is another of the legendary greats of the Golden Age of Piracy though it is unclear if he deserves the pirate label at all. William Kidd was convicted of murder and five counts of piracy before being hung twice (During the first execution the hanging rope broke before he had died. Youch!) but there is a lot of historical evidence that his was more of a political execution and that Kidd was really a privateer.

A privateer is something of a government-indorsed pirate. During times of war, they were allowed to board, raid, capture, and keep ships just as a pirate would, but only so long as the ships belonged to a foreigner. In some cases, a portion of the goods stolen, *er, appropriated* by the privateers would go back to the King or Queen that had authorized them in the first place (Queen Elizabeth would save England from bankruptcy in this way) but really the aim of sending out privateers was to interrupt the trading that the enemy so depended on.

Captain Kidd seems to be even more of a mythological creation than Blackbeard has ended up being. There are as many stories of his grand treasure as there are about his piracy, even though historians are as doubtful of the treasure as his profession. Kidd, whether a pirate or a privateer, does not seem to have been a very successful one. But that has stopped absolutely no one from looking for his treasure on Appledore Island.

Philip Babb had left the crew of Captain Kidd to become a respectable citizen. But in death he is a near demonic presence on the island, with glowing red eyes and a menacing air. He is sometimes accompanied by an unnamed ghost who is also thought to be a former Kidd crew member. Legend says the pair are guarding Kidd's treasure which he buried here as he dropped Babb off.

But another legend linked to this island makes it seem as if the treasure has already been found, if with frightful results. At one time, a butcher lived on the island who had a reputation that would have put that of the most bloodthirsty pirates to shame. The ill tempered man was found one day staggering around Appledore Island and raving about pirates' gold. Neighbors calmed him down and, over the course of a few weeks, were able to piece the story together.

One day while out walking, the butcher said he saw an old chest deep down in a steaming stinking hole created by two large pieces of granite. Intrigued by the unusual place he'd found, the butcher began trying to dig the chest up. It was wedged firmly in place. But in his efforts to dislodge the chest he broke part of the lid off. Inside it was filled with gleaming gold coins. Now convinced he had found the treasure of Captain Kidd the butcher began to work double time to get the chest out before anyone else happened along and found it.

The heat and exhaustion got to him. He was near crazed by the time his neighbors found him and he died within a few weeks. The neighbors, of course, searched the island diligently. They never found a chest, gold, or anyplace that looked remotely like the sulfurous hole described by the man.

MARIE ANTOINETTE'S NECKLACE

Everyone loves tales about lost loot. That's part of the reason why even the most outlandish stories involving gold and riches live on despite what history says otherwise about them. Do you believe that pirates gold might be found in New Hampshire? Sure. Well, maybe. But what about a spectacular diamond necklace created and owned by one of the most extravagant Queens in history? If it seems like a stretch, you might be surprised to find out there is a greater case for this lost treasure than for any of the pirate loot.

Marie Antoinette, unfairly or not, has gone down as one of history's worst and most extravagant Queens. She was the youngest child of Francis I, Holy Roman Emperor, and Maria Theresa, the Empress of Austria. She was Archduchess of Austria when, at the age of fourteen, she married Louis-Auguste and became the dauphin of France. When Kind Louis XV died in 1774, she became Queen of France and Navarre.

Both Marie and her husband would be executed during the French Revolution. She was an all-around despised figure. She was an Austrian, she had failed to produce the type of healthy male heir the French people wanted (her two sons were sickly creatures who both died before the age of ten), and she lived in unimaginable luxury while the people of France starved.

It is one of these luxury items that is said to have ended up lost just outside of Nashua, New Hampshire. In 1788, Marie Antoinette commissioned the finest jewelry makers of France to create the most lavish diamond necklace in the world. Marie, it seemed, wanted to be the envy of every Royal lady on the planet. Her jewelers scoured the globe to find the largest finest stones possible and they consulted every fine artisan in Europe on the design. At the time it was being created, no one could have imagined that in just five short years Marie Antoinette would be dead and the idea of Royalty would be anathema to the French people.

When things finally went bad for the Royal family, they went bad fast. Seeing the writing on the wall, Marie Antoinette packed up the dresses, the furniture, and the fabulous jewelry that she felt she just could not live without and had them sent by boat to Canada. There they were split up and stashed away with families who were good, upstanding Royalist sympathizers. To keep them safe, the items were constantly on the move. In 1790, one of these nondescript wooden trunks would begin traveling with a Frenchman and a Native American from Quebec into the United States.

The unusual duo made it as far as Nashua when they abruptly hauled out into the woods and built a secluded cabin. They came into town only rarely, taking turns, and garnered a reputation as hermits. In a few years, the Native started to make short trips back to Canada to visit with the family and friends he left behind. While he was gone the Frenchman became even more reclusive, shunning all visitors, and refusing to go into town even when he was in sore need of supplies.

Things continued this way for years. Finally, on one return trip, the Native found his friend dead, apparently from pneumonia. He packed up their belongings, closed up the cabin for good and left for his native lands.

Out of the blue, he would return ten years later. He hung around Nashua asking odd questions and roaming the woods at night. No one in town could figure out what he was doing. Finally, people began to complain. The local sheriff interrupted him on one of these midnight treks and hauled him into jail for questioning. After several weeks in the prison, and one assumes under duress, he told his tale. Years after returning home, he had reason to go through the belongings he'd brought back from the cabin. In his friends journal he found a notation, written when the man realized he was deathly ill, that he had buried the wooden chest near the river by the cabin and rolled a large stone over it to mark the spot. When the sheriff asked the man what was inside the chest that was so important he came all this way after all this time to find it he was told the chest contained the belongings of Marie Antoinette. In particular inside the wooden box was an ornate metal case holding her famed diamond necklace.

Mysteriously, the Native would disappear soon after. The sheriff put out word that he had been released and had returned home but in time, once his story began to spread, people began to wonder if something more sinister had happened to the man.

And the story did spread. The sheriff searched quietly for the necklace for months. He could find the remains of the cabin. He could find the river near the cabin. But, well, New Hampshire isn't called the Granite State for nothing. He spent months rolling over every boulder he found but there were just too darn many of them. Eventually, he had to start telling people what he was looking for in order to get their help to find it.

People continue to search to this day. Marie Antoinette's necklace has never been found, in New Hampshire, or anywhere else.

Ocean Born Mary

The pirate held the screaming newborn baby in one hand and walked slowly up and down the deck of the ship. The child's parents, clearly expecting the worst, huddled fearfully along with the rest of the passengers.

The year was 1720, it was a bad time for ocean voyages, and the trip had been made even more dangerous for Elizabeth Fulton when she gave birth mid-trip. But her baby, a girl, was strong and healthy and chances seemed good that mother and child would have no trouble surviving the trip. That's when the watch called out that pirates were closing in fast. Then everything began happening with frightful speed. The pirates had overtaken their ship, come aboard, and relieved the terrified immigrants of any valuables they might have had in what seemed like minutes. Elizabeth had only a spare second to try and save her newborn daughter. She hid the baby as best she could and prayed it would be enough. It wasn't. While ransacking the cargo, looking for things that could used or sold, the pirate captain himself heard the small noises of the child that soon developed

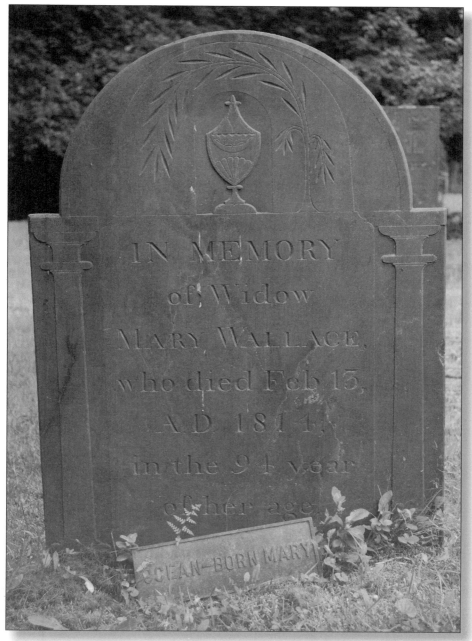

The grave of Mary Wallace can be found in the Old Center Cemetery in Henniker, the same town as the famous Ocean Born Mary House

into full-fledged wails as he brought her into the crisp ocean air and demanded to see her parents.

Afraid of angering the pirate, Elizabeth and her husband stepped forward timidly and claimed the baby as their own. The pirate stared at them for a few moments, as if deciding something.

"I will let everyone aboard this vessel live," he declared. "*If you will name this baby after my mother, Mary.*"

It was such an unbelievable bargain that everyone feared it was a trick but Elizabeth was willing to grasp whatever straws of hope that were thrown her way. She instantly agreed and, to the surprise of everyone including the crew of the pirate ship,

Mary Wallace's tombstone in no way indicates her status as a local legend so this small plaque was added to the grave years after he death.

the Captain kept his word. Before returning to his own ship, its cargo hold full with stolen goods, the Captain ordered a full bolt of bright green brocade cloth be given to the young parents of little Mary.

"For her wedding gown," the Pirate called out flippantly. "For when the time comes for her to marry."

Infant Mary thrived in New Hampshire, years passed and she grew into a red-haired Irish beauty. And when the time came, she threw aside tradition and turned up her nose at the usual virginal white dress. Instead she was married in a dress crafted from the green pirate's brocade her parents had been presented with so many years before.

There are two tales that are New England's most popular, and persistent, pieces of folklore. One is the story of Jonathan Moulton and his ill-fated deal with the Devil, which can be found in the next chapter in this book. The others are the stories about Ocean Born Mary. Like Jonathan Moulton, Mary was very much a real person. The facts of her life are well known and, for the time, well documented. However, whatever facts we know about Mary are usually ignored in favor of the legends that have been built up around her. The story of her birth at sea, and near brush with death at the hands of what turned out to be very generous pirates, are just the start of the Ocean Born Mary folklore. Extended versions of the legend of her life include the pirate who spared her life so many years before returning to New Hampshire to claim her as his wife (in reality Mary wed James Wallace, definitely not a pirate, in 1742, and remained a widow after his death at the ripe old age of 81). Others say that the pirate came back to the Granite state when he retired from sea, that he built a fabulous house near that of one of Mary's sons, and that he hired her as a housekeeper (she would have been better off as a pirate's wife, unless of course the pirate happened to be Bluebeard). Some say that the pirate returned just to give Mary a treasure chest full of gold doubloons that she never spent and instead secreted away somewhere around the town of Henniker.

There is even an Ocean Born Mary tourist attraction of a sort, the Ocean Born Mary House. In 1917, a Wisconsin businessman decided to relocate to New Hampshire with his mother. Louis Roy put out word that he was in the market for an old home that had an interesting history attached to it. An enterprising Henniker postal worker told Roy the story of Ocean Born Mary and pointed out an oversized colonial home in town that he said had been her house. Roy loved it. He loved it so much in fact that he decided it didn't matter in the least that Mary had never actually lived in the house. Roy charged visitors for a tour of his new home, supplied some tantalizing remarks about the treasure chest of gold buried, he was quite sure, somewhere in the nearby orchard, and never thought to mention that the house had been owned by one of Mary's three sons – not Mary. Mary had actually lived with a different son, several miles further down the road.

The lore about Mary Wallace's birth, her life, and even her place of residence are so firmly entrenched, it has even extended to stories about her afterlife. The Ocean Born Mary House (the one she did not live in) is said to be haunted by her ghost. The ghost stories began, perhaps not surprisingly, shortly after Roy bought the home and began trying to market it as an attraction. Roy and his mother Flora were, they said, both convinced that Mary was a protective force in and around the house. They credited her spirit for staying Roy's hand when he inadvertently was about a throw a small bag containing gunpowder in the fireplace, for urging him out of a garage that was about to collapse, and to protecting the house from the ravages of a hurricane. All in all, the Roys said they had missed death a good seventeen times and had survived, in one way or another, thanks to a spectral lady in a old-fashioned white dress.

Many would-be ghost hunters and amateur psychics have also claimed, over the years, to have sensed Mary in the house. At one point, two New Hampshire state troopers reported seeing a spectral red-headed woman hovering along the road outside the home. The couple who took over the home after the death of Louis Roy encouraged the stories. But, after several years of giving interviews and publicizing their paranormal experiences with Mary, they abruptly recanted the ghost stories. The current owners of the still-famous Ocean Born Mary House are quite adamant that there are no ghosts and have tried to get the word out that Mary never lived in their home. But, like most things about Mary's life, the truth doesn't matter in the least. People take nearly as many pictures of the home, and knock on the door asking for a tour, as they did back in the Roy's day.

JONATHAN MOULTON MAKES A DEAL WITH THE DEVIL

Already a military man of some note, having fought in King George's War, the French and Indian War as well as the Revolutionary War, husband to a loving wife, and having achieved much fame and fortune as a businessman, most Hampton residents would have said that Jonathan Moulton had everything any man could want. But Jon Moulton wanted more. Sitting in front of the fire one snowy evening he found himself musing on what he could do with an even greater wealth than what he already had. Half asleep, already dreaming of luxuries he did not already possess, it occurred to Moulton that, just perhaps, it would be worth it to trade his soul for unlimited riches.

At that very instant, a shower of sparks exploded from the living room fireplace. Moulton, instantly awake, jumped from his rocking chair expecting to see fire break out in his respectably decorated home. What he found instead was even more alarming. Stepping out of the still burning fire place was a tall thin man clad in a suit made entirely of rich black velvet.

"Greetings Mr. Moulton," said the gentleman in a cultured oddly accented voice. "I heard you were interested in a bargain."

Jonathan Moulton took several steps back, half falling over his rocking chair. The strange man watched him calmly and Moulton noticed, feeling feverish, that smoldering coals seemed to burn in the visitor's eyes.

"Who . . .who are you?" stammered the normally fearless General. "You can't be the . . . well, the . . ."

"Hush now Mr. Moulton," said the man. Though his smile never faltered, he silenced Moulton with his threatening look. "Names don't matter. Not between friends. But I am in a hurry and don't have time for chatter. Do we have a deal or not?"

Up to now, Jonathan Moulton had been too frightened to think straight, but at the word *deal* he began to consider things a little more calmly. By this time in his life, Moulton was already known as a shrewd businessman. Ironically, he had often been heard bragging that neither man nor devil could get the better of him in a business deal. If there was anyone who could match their savvy with the devil and come out on top, Jon Moulton felt he was that man. But at the same time Moulton had always been God fearing, a regular at church, and respected by his neighbors. Did he dare risk all that, on top of his immortal soul, for a little bit of money?

The Devil said nothing while Moulton thought this through. He looked once at pocket watch, though not impatiently, and casually began to go through the contents of his coat pockets. Just as Moulton began to hesitate a stream of pure gold coins fell, as if by accident, from the pockets of the velvet suit.

All thoughts of refusing fled from Moulton's head as he dived to the floor to grab up the coins. The first he touched burned his hand. He yelped and yanked his hand back, looking for a blister. Too his surprise his hand was unmarked, no blisters and no red spots showing where he was burned. The man in the velvet suit laughed gently and motioned that he should go back to scooping up the coins. Moulton paused for only a second before gently touching one finger to the gleaming gold coin. He found it cool to the touch. Instantly Moulton started scooping up coins stuffing them into the pockets of his robe.

While the General scrabbled around the floorboards at his feet the visitor pulled a piece of parchment from his coat and began to write. When all the coins were gone the Devil gently tapped Moulton on the shoulder and showed him the paper.

"Sign here and on the first night of every month I'll fill your boots with gold coins just like the ones you just placed in your robe."

Moulton instantly reached for the contract and pen. Just as he was about to touch them the Devil yanked them out of reach. Holding the parchment behind his back he looked at Moulton with grave sadness.

"Mark my words before you sign, Jon Moulton," he intoned deeply. "If you try to trick me you'll come out the worse for it. I've heard you bragging and I know how your mind works. I'll be keeping my eye on you and this is the only warning you'll get."

Moulton nodded quickly, reaching for the contract again, though he couldn't look the Devil in the eyes when he did. Moulton told himself it was because it was too unnerving to see those smoldering red globes burning hotly in the man's otherwise handsome face but he was just lying to himself. The truth was that he had already been scheming how to get more than the offered two bootfuls of gold from the Devil each month.

Moulton signed and the deal was complete. The Devil kept to his end of the bargain. As each month rolled around Moulton placed his boots next to the fireplace and the next morning he found them filled to the brim with gold coins. Moulton's wealth grew so quickly and so noticeably that it soon became the talk of Hampton. Neighbors didn't know what was stranger, the sudden unexplainable wealth of the Moulton family or Moulton's sudden interest in larger and larger types of boots. He began simply enough, purchasing larger sizes in the style of boots he already owned. Then he realized that his deal only specified that boots be placed by the fireplace—there were no clauses saying what kind of boots he had to use. Moulton finally settled on an extra large pair of military issue jack-boots that reached him at mid-thigh. Moulton had to admit he had a sleepless night the first time he put those out by the fireplace. But the next morning they were filled with gold, same as all the other pairs of boots. The Devil, Moulton reasoned, was busy—either too busy to notice the size of his boots or too busy to care if he did notice.

It never occurred to Moulton that perhaps the devil was lulling him into false sense of security, letting him back himself into a corner there would be no way to talk himself out of.

One would think that eventually Moulton would have all the gold he could have needed. But it seemed the more he got, the more he wanted to get. . . and the more daring he became. Finally, he struck on a truly outlandish idea. One evening he cut the soles from the bottom of his boots, placed them next to the fireplace as usual, and then drilled holes through the floorboards beneath them. Now the boots looked normal enough, but really acted like funnels into the cavernous basement of his home. Moulton was pleased with his ingenuity and went happily off to bed.

That night the devil came, same as he did the first of every month and started pouring coins into the boots. He poured and poured and still they would not fill. Vexed he poured faster but still he could not fill the shoes. Furious he gave them a good strong kick. They fell over and instantly the Devil could see how Moulton had tried to trick him. As the Devil became angrier and angrier the gold coins within the basement turned white hot with his fury and the floorboards began to smoke. Soon the fine silk curtains on the windows started to smolder and the Devil took his leave.

Moulton's home, known as Hampton House, burned to the ground that night. The next day Moulton dug through the ashes hoping desperately to find some of the gold coins but the ruins of the basement were filled with nothing more valuable than rubble and even the gold that he had secreted away against tough times was gone.

But all was not lost for Jon Moulton. Long before he began making deals with the Devil he was already a wealthy businessman, having started his own import business, and having been granted enormous tracts of land for his exemplary service in the French and Indian War. In quick order the fortune's of Jon Moulton were looking up again. That does not mean, of course, that all of Moulton's worries were over. He had, after explicitly being told not to, tried to pull a fast one over on Lucifer himself. But as time went on, his memories of the incident faded. The Devil never came back and things were only looking up for Jon, his wife Abigail, and their eleven children.

Several years after the fire that decimated their home, Moulton's wife Abigail contracted a mysterious illness. Doctors were called from all over New England to try and diagnose the cause of her mysterious wasting away, even though by this time Moulton was said to have become tired of his wife. But none could explain or cure her ailment. After a few months with no recovery in sight, Moulton contacted his wife's dearest friend, Sarah Emery, and asked her to come help him care for the dying Abigail.

Sarah Emery was young and outgoing; she breathed new life into the rebuilt walls of Hampton House. Long before Abigail passed on, Hampton residents were talking about a possible love affair between Sarah and Jon. It was said that the old General took her out to fine Boston restaurants and lavished her with gifts. But, a frugal Yankee despite his massive wealth, Jonathan was said to have taken the jewels he gave to his mistress straight from the jewelry box of his dying wife.

The talk around town was only validated when, less than a year after Abigail's death, Sarah Emery became Sarah Moulton. Jonathan became roaringly drunk at the festivities, passing out drunk in the downstairs parlor. Sarah spent her wedding night crying upstairs. Through her sobs, she heard footsteps coming up the stairs and hopefully dried her eyes. Perhaps her husband, she thought hopefully, had not been as drunk as he seemed.

But when the bedroom door opened her hopeful smile froze on her face. Instead of her sheepish bridegroom coming to apologize, Sarah saw the misty figure of her former best friend float towards her, fury in her eyes. Sarah threw her hands in front of her, trying to keep the ghost away, and felt icy hands grip her own. She began to scream, finally passing out.

When she came to, her husband still downstairs oblivious to what had happened upstairs, all her jewelry was gone. Even the beautiful wedding band, second hand from Abigail of course, Jonathan had placed on her finger in front of all their friends and neighbors early in the day was gone. Neither the jewelry, nor Abigail's spirit, were seen again.

Sarah and General Moulton would make it through their rough first few days of married life and have nearly a dozen years of wedded bliss before Moulton's death in 1787. His funeral would be one of the largest Hampton would ever see. But as the casket was carried from the church to the cemetery for burial, an accident would mar the solemnity of the day. One of the pallbearers tripped, dropping his corner of the casket, which promptly popped open as it fell to the ground. Instantly a scream of horror ripped through the mourners. Inside the silk-lined coffin, there was no body. Instead mourners were shocked to see a tide of gold coins spill out, each and every one stamped with the grinning visage of Satan himself.

Like all good stories, there are some elements of truth in these legends. To begin with, Jonathan Moulton was a real person who was born in, and spent most of his life in, Hampton during the

1700s. Originally apprenticed to a cabinet maker, Moulton would leave this trade and join the New Hampshire militia at the age of nineteen. The young Moulton made a name for himself as a soldier in King George's War. It was towards the end of this war that he met his first wife, Abigail, with whom he would go on to have eleven children, and started his first business. Further, Moulton did very well for himself. He built a fine home known as Hampton House and filled it with many luxurious goods imported from Europe and the West Indies. We can only assume that it was this spectacular rise from simple cabinet maker to prominent local businessman that started tongues wagging throughout his hometown. Surely the Moutons lifestyle wasn't the product of hard work and sacrifice—he must have made a deal with the Devil.

Moulton's original Hampton House did burn down, just as in the legend about Jon Moulton. The fire began in the early hours of the morning on March 15, 1769. Between all of the Moulton children, servants, and visitors, there were close to thirty people in the house when the fire began. They were extremely lucky to have all escaped uninjured. No cause was ever found for the blaze.

Hampton House was rebuilt, using as many of the original bricks as possible. And years later, Abigail Moulton did mysteriously sicken and die . . . just to be replaced a year later with her best friend, Sarah Emery. But sometimes fact is more interesting than fiction. While the coffin filled with gold coins is only part myth, there is some evidence that his body may have disappeared before burial. But technically, that can't be proven one way or another. Jonathan Moulton's grave is empty. No one knows for sure what became of the famed General's body; he is the only high-ranking Revolutionary War hero in New Hampshire whose grave site is unknown. It is truly an unusual ending for a Revolutionary War hero who considered George Washington a personal friend.

The Moulton mythology continues to be added onto to this day. Hampton House, the second one at least, does still exist and is reported to be heavily haunted. People have been seeing ghosts roaming the stately hallways since Moulton's time. In more recent years, owners of the home have been so disturbed by ghostly happenings and the links to the Devil, legendary or not, they had an exorcism performed over the house.

Curious Creatures

Cryptozoology is the study of animals whose existence is not accepted by the larger scientific community. Many of these creatures are mythological in nature or stem from local folklore. Legitimate science denies the existence of such creatures. Depending on your beliefs, this might be because the creatures do not exist at all outside of stories or, if you are a believer, that they are so special and so rare as to not commonly be seen by humans. Famous creatures most often studied by cryptozoologists include such tabloid favorites as Bigfoot or Nessie from Scotland's Loch Ness. A few of these kinds of creatures are rumored to be found here in New Hampshire.

Wood Devil

In and around the woods surrounding Berlin many people over the years have sighted something strange. This creature, known locally as the Wood Devil, seems to be a close relative of the rather famous creature said by some to frequent the Pacific Northwest. Could New Hampshire have its very own Bigfoot?

Some people certainly think it's possible. Native American tribes across the country talked about Bigfoot-like creatures long before white settlers arrived in America. Different tribes assigned them different names, of course, but when their meaning is translated many of these names are startlingly similar; Timber Giants, the Hairy Man, the One Who Runs and Hides, etc. These names do a pretty good job of describing the appearance and personality of the creature that today is most commonly known as Bigfoot.

Settlers to New Hampshire's North Country also told tales of mysterious creatures, dubbing them Wood Devils. Despite the Satanic moniker, the Wood Devils are frightening only in their appearance and not in their actions. While many, many encounters with Wood Devils have been reported over the years, there are no known reports of the creatures trying to inflict harm on the witnesses. The Wood Devil is described as being very tall, close to eight feet, incredibly thin, with long tangled hair covering its grayish skin and the requisite oversized feet. The Wood Devil walks upright on two legs, and can move quite quickly on them when surprised, and, while more or less human shaped, it has no neck. The creature's large oval head sits directly on top of its shoulders. Now imagine being surprised by something like that while out in the woods and you can see why they frighten people!

The Wood Devil has a piercing shriek that seems to be used to scare off people who approach it. Most often the creature tries to hide when it inadvertently comes near humans. With its camouflage of dark hair, the creature can also freeze behind a tree when it sees humans.

Reports of Wood Devil sightings continue to this day. Each fall many deer hunters walk out of the woods near Berlin and declare they will never walk back in. While not menaced by the Wood Devil, just seeing it is enough to warn them off. Other people have less close encounters. The oversized tracks of the animal have been found more often than the animal itself.

THE DERRY TROLL

What would your first impulse be if you came across a legendary or mythological creature? Would you be afraid? Would you run? With cameras built into everything from cell phones to handheld video game systems, and high prices being offered by collectors and the media for "proof" of formerly unfound creatures, these days most peoples' first idea would be to take a picture. One thing is for certain though, it would take a very brave, or very foolish, person to approach an inexplicable critter and try to catch it barehanded.

But that is precisely what one man from Derry did when confronted with a living breathing mystery. On December 15, 1956, while out in the woods chopping down Christmas trees for sale, one Derry resident was confronted by a two-foot-tall, wrinkly, green, vaguely human-shaped creature—though it was about as far from one of Santa's elves as a small green man could be! The creature's skin was thick and rough looking, its body blocky and ill formed, and it had two long floppy ears drooping down the sides of its misshapen bald head.

Rather than running away, which would have been a perfectly understandable response to seeing a deformed looking Christmas elf while in the woods, the man decided to catch the creature. Reasoning that no one would believe his tale without the actual troll there as proof, the man leapt up from where he'd been spying on the creature and ran madly towards it. As soon as the troll saw the man coming towards him, it gave out a wild piercing screech (which is, really, a perfectly understandable reaction on the part of the troll). Suddenly aware that he was chasing an inexplicable creature through the woods, the man realized his folly and ran away for home.

If this was a singular tale about something unexplained living in Derry, it would be easy to disregard this one anecdote as attention seeking or a prank. But, long before this Christmas season encounter, both earlier Scottish-Irish settlers and the Native Americans before them told tales of fairy or elf-like creatures in and around what is now Derry. The Native Americans even had a name, location, and leader of this tribe of small unusual people. They believed that the "elves" lived around what is today called Beaver Lake. The tribe was led by a Queen of sorts called Tsienneto (or Neto for short). There are many conflicting stories about Neto and her tribe that come from both the Natives and the Scots. In some they are a protective force, helping those in extreme duress; in others, they cause not harm exactly, but are the perpetrators of all sorts of malicious pranks.

If it were not for the more modern day encounter these stories would undoubtedly be taken as pure myth. But with the account from the 1950s included, it is at least possible to consider that the myths had a little less to do with pure imagination then first suspected.

THE STONE-THROWING DEVIL

The night of June 11, 1682 began normal enough in New Castle. That is, it was a typical night for everyone on the tiny island town except for the Walton family. The prominent family was just closing up their tavern home when a thunder of what sounded like hail was heard beating down mercilessly on their home. As they rushed outside to see the source of the noise they were dumbfounded.

The house was being pelted mercilessly, but it wasn't rain and it wasn't hail. Falling from the skies with frightening intensity were rocks. Some of the stones were, thankfully, as small as pebbles. Others were fist sized stones that left a good bruise if they happened to hit you The sound of the stone flurry whacking on the roof of the Walton's home was so loud that neighbors began to hear the din. Word of the odd occurrence made its way through town like wildfire and people rushed to the Walton's to see the weird weather phenomenon with their own eyes.

The Waltons fled inside, as much to get away from the curious as from the rocks. But their home was no longer the shelter it previously was. Besides being the building on the island that was being singled out for some kind of obscure rock-related weather phenomenon, it was now raining inside as well as out. They were surprised to run inside and find several inches of stones covering their previously bare floors and, more disturbing still, not one window was open or broken, so they knew the stone showering was happening inside the home, not just coming in from outside.

Furious, George Walton, the patriarch of the Walton family, began rushing around the outside of the home mindless of the rocks he was being hit with. He was sure it was some kind of elaborate prank and that soon he would find whomever was throwing rocks at his house, and how. But days went by, the rocks continued to fall, and no culprit could be found. As far as anyone could tell, the rocks were falling out of the sky, not being thrown or catapulted from somewhere else.

George Walton became obsessed with what was happening to his family. He moved his children away to try and protect them from the inexplicable happenings and the attention it was garnering, but no matter where they went a rain of stones followed right behind them. At another point George gathered together a pile of stones, painted them white, and locked them away in a secret location. Not long afterwards a rain of white painted stones started up and when he checked the ones he had hidden, he found them gone. It defied all logic and scientific inquiry.

As you can imagine, the weather problems that followed the family was big news back in 1682, just as much as it would be today. The family was very well thought of in town, and the notion of them trying to pull off such an elaborate hoax was unthinkable. On top of their outstanding reputations, much of the Walton family troubles were witnessed by Richard Chamberlain, who was secretary of the colony of New Hampshire at the time. He was an adamant supporter of the family, and the authenticity of the bizarre occurrences happening to them. With such a prestigious witness on scene, it was not long before scientists came from all over the country, and all over the world, to either find a rational explanation for the problem or to debunk the Walton's outright. Every last one of them would leave confused and angry when one after another their experiments failed to produce results. The scientist could not come up with even one theory that the rocks didn't defy.

The fall of rocks was, and remains to this day, to be a mystery.

Eventually, the fall of rocks ended. It didn't taper off or fade; as suddenly as it had started, it stopped. With no scientific explanation to be found, and with the reputations of the Waltons and their supporters considered unimpeachable, it was finally decided that witchcraft could be the only explanation. An old woman who lived near the family was accused. In general the town people, and the wider world at large who had taken interest in the family's troubles, seemed satisfied with that conclusion.

LAKAWAKA

Traditionally in Ireland and Scotland all funerary rights included a lyke wake and a lyke walk. The lyke wake came as soon as the deceased passed on. Their family would prepare the body for viewing and open their own home to friends and neighbors who wanted to come and pay their respects. During this extended wake period, the corpse was never left alone—not when an extended family member came calling and certainly not in the middle of the night while the rest of the town slept. This was the lyke wake, the watching of the corpse by a trusted family member, most often a woman, to guard against possession by dark forces or to make sure that the deceased's spirit didn't try to reclaim their body.

What is probably the world's strangest lyke wake is said to have taken place off the coast of New Hampshire during the 1800s. The seas around the Isles of Shoals, the collection of small islands shared by New Hampshire and Maine, had long been known to harbor a sea monster. Stories of this enormous worm-like creature had been told by everyone from the early settlers of the region to the original Native American inhabitants, and everyone had a different name for the normally shy and reclusive creature. But reports of a glowing segmented worm around the waters off the Shoals unexpectedly ramped up in the early 1800s. It was Scottish immigrants who first recognized what the creature was doing and ultimately came to give the monster its longest lasting name.

The creature was, the Scots said, sitting in lyke wake for its mate. From this the name Lakawaka was born. Lakawaka would be seen very infrequently after the wake period for its mate was over and there have been no reports of the creature for the past hundred years or so. Lakawaka it seems may have passed on itself with no mate to watch over its body and leaving no children to astound the modern day sailors who roam around the Isles of Shoals.

THE SILVER MADONNA

Treasure hunters take note, there is a two-foot-tall solid-silver Virgin Mary on the loose in New Hampshire and we need your help finding it. You may have some competition though. Treasure hunters, casual and professional, consider this lost Mary to be one of the single most sought after treasures in the northeastern states.

Created by the Catholic Church, the Silver Madonna was then installed in a missionary church in a native Abenaki village in Quebec. This village was the site of a massacre at the beginning of the French and Indian War. British troops had been sent to sack the small village as part of the escalating violence that led to the war. In a shockingly short period of time, British troops killed over 200 people, every man, woman, and child in the village. Even the Catholic priest was not spared.

The troops descended on the church, prying gold-gilded frames off art work and stuffing the ornate chalices used to give communion into sacks. When they came across the silver Madonna, it must have seemed like a dream come true. She was pried up and tossed into the pile along with whatever other riches they could find.

The British troops were partway home when scouts rushed up to their commander, telling him a large party of French military men were on their way to avenge the massacred souls. The British, weighed down by two pack horses carting their stolen treasures decided to stay and fight. They got more of a fight than they bargained for. The land where they had decided to make their stand was ill suited for their purposes and local Native American tribes, stirred up by the killings at the Abenaki village, rushed to the aid of the French. Realizing they could not win this battle, the British leader ordered his men to split into two groups and make a quick retreat.

The French were not so easily thrown off. They also split their forces and decided to pursue the fleeing British. In all the confusion both pack horses, and all the gold, silver, and furs they had stolen, ended up with the same party of British troops instead of one with each group. This wouldn't be that big of a problem if the British had held ranks and met back up at the fort as they were supposed to, but with the continued pursuit of the French, and no doubt realizing they had a fortune in stolen goods, the one band deserted.

One Ranger, a man named Parsons, swore he knew the area very well and led his band of deserters towards New Hampshire. Near the Vermont border, one of the horses became lame under the weight of all the gold it was carrying. The men, still worried about the French troops somewhere behind them and with no other way to carry their ill gotten gold, left the horse and everything it carried. Parsons then led the men up north into the White Mountains.

With a staggering sum of money but not a single thing to eat or drink, the small group of men became almost instantly lost. Taking shelter beneath an outcropping of rock, they killed the horse to drink its blood and cut it up for meat. In their haste for food, the horse meat went largely uncooked and by the next morning they were all not only near starving, but deliriously sick.

In his derangement, Parsons decided that the silver Madonna was to blame for their troubles. He staggered away from the meager shelter he shared with three other men and hauled her from the packs where she was wrapped up for safe keeping. While the other men watched, either thinking they were hallucinating or just too weak to stop him, Parsons rolled the silver statue down the embankment where she splashed into a nearby river. Then, still crazed, he ran off into the woods never to be seen again.

The next morning when one of the men awoke in their rock shelter, he found his other companions dead, either from exhaustion, starvation, or disease. Somehow he was able to find his feet and begin walking. If the Madonna had cursed them, than her watery burial must have broken it because, against all odds, the man reached a very small settlement that afternoon. The townsfolk took him in and nursed him back to health. While he recovered, he told them his tale.

The townspeople weren't sure whether or not to believe the story. A group of men set out from the town and started to walk along the Israel River in hopes of finding some of the landmarks the man had told them about. Eventually they did find, under a shallow outcropping of rock, the bodies of two British soldiers. Nearby were the bones of a slain horse and a few scattered gold and silver artifacts. They checked the river but were never able to find the statue.

Since then, many people have tried their hand at finding the lost silver Madonna. The river where she was so unceremoniously rolled still winds its slow course through the mountains. It is known for its incredibly muddy bottom. Between the weight of the silver statue and the amount of silt that must have covered her in all the years that have passed, she is well hidden.

THE VISITORS

Interestingly enough, New Hampshire and UFOs have a long shared history. The oldest known UFO photograph in existence was taken atop Mount Washington in 1870. The old photo, famous among UFO enthusiasts, shows the white billowing clouds that are typical of the summit of Mount Washington. In the center of these clouds is a distinct dark gray cigar-shaped object. The photo caused a sensation when it was first taken and it remains unexplained to this day.

THE HILL INCIDENT

But New Hampshire's most famous UFO incident took place nearly a hundred years later. Betty and Barney Hill, a Portsmouth couple, were returning home from a road trip throughout upstate New York and Quebec. The highway was deserted, this being late September when the summer people had gone home for the season and it being too late at night for leaf peepers. Both Betty and Barney noticed a particularly bright star that seemed to be following them. Barney reasoned that is must be a satellite that only appeared to be on their tails, but Betty had noticed the light moving peculiarly, hovering around the moon and back down again. She asked her husband to stop the car, ostensibly so she could give their dog a bathroom break, but really because she wanted to use the binoculars to get a closer look at the light.

Stepping outside the car, Betty got a clearer view of the craft, seeing for the first time that it was covered in multi-colored flashing lights. Not knowing much about the aircraft of the day, she was not yet frightened, she was curious about what she was seeing but did not yet have an inkling of the bizarre turn her life was about to take.

The Hills started back up the highway, driving slower so they could watch the antics of the light. It zipped around mountains, flew quickly towards the Hill's car, and then away again in an instant. Barney began to worry that it was some type of top secret military craft and that they might be in trouble for witnessing its test flight. His worries took a back seat to flat out horror when the craft rapidly descended directly towards their car, forcing him to stop abruptly in the middle of the empty highway.

The Hills stepped outside their vehicle, Barney grabbing the binoculars his wife had discarded earlier. It was obvious to them both now that what they were seeing was something out of this world. The craft held position, as if considering the couple, and Barney saw nearly a dozen vaguely humanoid creatures peering at them through the craft's windows.

"They're trying to capture us!" Barney shrieked at his wife, who was standing as if frozen on the other side of the vehicle.

His voice broke whatever was holding her enthralled. In one quick motion they dashed back to their car and jumped inside. Barney slammed his foot down on the gas and the car jumped forward. Betty looked around the sky but the craft seemed to have disappeared.

But the strange happenings were not so easily over for the Hills. This encounter was just the beginning. As they traveled a few more miles down the road, keeping a keen eye out for lights in the sky to be sure, they started to hear a weird beeping noise come from the trunk of their car. As soon as the noise began both Betty and Barney felt a tingling sensation moving through their bodies even as they had to struggle to keep their eyes open. Utter exhaustion washed through them even though they had felt very awake up to this point.

The Hills reached their home around 5:30 that morning—very odd considering the trip should have resulted in them getting home no later than one o'clock. There was some other odd occurrences at their home as well. Betty, for no reason she could think of, felt compelled to keep her luggage near the back door leading from the house rather than bringing it inside where it belonged. They discovered that the tough leather strap on their binoculars was torn straight through even though neither of them could remember how it could have happened. Also torn was Betty's dress, which along with her shoes was covered in a pink tinted powder. Betty suggested that she and her husband each draw a picture of the object they had seen in the sky that night and a timeline of events. Both were startled to discover their memories of the night were fragmented, didn't match up with each others, and made no sense considering the incredible length of time it took for them to get home that evening. Their drawings of the craft however matched exactly.

A few days later, upset by the encounter and their increasingly disjointed memories of what happened, Betty called the local Air Force base to report what had happened to them. Patronizingly, Betty was told that she must have misidentified the planet Jupiter. But that is not to say that, no matter what they made out to the Hills, the Air Force wasn't taking their report at least a little seriously. They had picked up strange anomalies on their radar screens that evening, right around the same time as the Hills were having their run in with whatever it was on that highway. The report Betty gave the Air Force was, though they didn't know it at the time, forwarded along to Project Blue Book.

Project Blue Book was one in a series of studies about UFOs done by the United States Air Force. The main goals of the study were to look into the possibility that alien spacecraft did exist, did sometimes visit Earth, and to decide how much of a threat these visitors might be. Altogether Project Blue Book collected over

12,000 reports of likely alien encounters. When the project ended in the 1960s, they declared authoritatively that the reports they had collected were misidentifications of planets, that aliens most likely did not exist, and that if they did, they were no threat to the United States. The U.S. Air Force, they said, was done spending money and time on UFO research. That being said many people did not believe the official word that came down from the Air Force. Even today, many people believe that there are top secret studies similar to Project Blue Book being conducted by some department of the United States military and/or government, or that Project Blue Book did find definitive proof that aliens existed and were part of a massive governmental cover up to keep this information from the public.

Betty Hill spent the next few days after giving her report doing some research of her own. The Portsmouth Public Library didn't have many non-fiction books about alien encounters. For that matter, there weren't many books on the topic, period, in the Portsmouth Library or not. This was 1961, and alien abductions weren't given nearly any of the attention they receive today. One of the books that Betty did find, that seemed most credible to her after her own experience, was written by a retired Marine Major who now worked with a private sector UFO research group known as the National Investigations Committee on Aerial Phenomena (or NICAP). Excited at the prospect of being taken seriously, and increasingly disturbed by the nightmares created by the incident, Betty contacted NICAP and set up a time to be interviewed.

NICAP spent six hours interviewing the Hills on this first session, significantly more than the half hour the Air Force has spent on the phone with Betty. This would be just the first of countless interviews between NICAP and the Hills. NICAP was able to confirm for Betty that what they had experienced was very typical in alien abduction cases. While this seemed to help calm Betty's lingering fears about the incident, it only increased Barney's anxiety. He was still not one hundred percent sure that what they had experienced was linked to an extraterrestrial race, but Betty was a firm believer by this point.

Within a few years of the incident, the Hills, supported by NICAP, went public with what they had experienced. It created a media frenzy. In this day and age, stories of alien encounters are, if not common, at least a known factor. Whether you are a believer in UFOs, or if you pass these stories off as tabloid trash, even the casual news reader comes across these types of accounts from time to time. This was decidedly not the case in the 1960s. People did not talk about alien abductions, newspapers did not report on such exotic news, and movies and books were only written on the subject if they were fictional accounts in comic books written for children.

Betty and Barney Hill changed all of that. They were open about what they had experienced. They welcomed whatever scientific study anyone was willing to do to verify or discredit their story. The dress Betty wore that evening would undergo chemical testing. Both of the Hills would be hypnotized by a reputable Boston psychiatrist. Betty and Barney were average middle-class people, well educated, upstanding citizens, important figures in their local church. They were exactly not the type of people who would normally admit to a brush with the uncanny.

The Hill's encounter would capture international attention. Betty, the more outspoken of the couple and the more definite about it being an alien abduction, would become a minor celebrity not just to the UFO community but to the world at large. Several books and at least one movie would go on to be written about what has gone down in history as "The Hill Incident." It has been called the start of the modern age of UFO encounters.

A FLYING OBJECT

Every state has had UFO sightings, but New Hampshire has had more than its fair share, especially once you consider that it's the seventh smallest state in the nation. Most of the alien sightings that take place in the state seem to cluster in the Seacoast region, more specifically in Rockingham County. The Hills may be the most famous people to have met up with aliens in New Hampshire, but they are not the only ones by any means.

In July of 1951, two military personnel stationed in Portsmouth made a report that they had seen a long flying object that was a hundred feet or more in length and five times as wide as it was long. They had seen this object zipping around the night skies at unheard of speeds. The men, who should have been able to make an accurate estimate considering their own flying experience, said the object was flying at speeds exceeding a thousand miles an hour. It was made from a dull gray metal, speckled with dark spots, and left a bright glowing trail in its wake. The object was only visible for about a minute but they were both able to describe it in acute detail.

A Chase

One of the states more famous sightings took place in September of 1965. Only five people reported witnessing the event but two of them were Exeter police officers (and one of them a decorated Air Force veteran on top of that) so even non-believers were slightly more inclined to believe that something unexplainable by normal standards was going on.

A Navy recruiter named Norman Muscarella was walking home from his girlfriend's house when an object he later described as being larger than a good-sized house and covered in flashing red light loomed out of the clouds above him. Norman picked up his pace but the huge object made its way to directly over him. The craft started to wobble, slowly descending towards Norman until he panicked and threw himself into the ditch running alongside the road. When he looked up the UFO was gone.

Understandably frantic, Norman flagged down the next car that passed by on the road and asked to be taken to the Exeter police station. There Officer Eugene Bertrand took down the complaint. Normally he would have just passed it off as a prank of some sort but he gave Norman's account more credence because a young woman had just left the police station who reported a similar object in the same area that had, she said, chased her car for twelve miles before zipping off into the night.

Norman and Bertrand jumped into a police cruiser with Norman acting as navigator. They returned to the stretch of road where Norman had first encountered the craft. The skies were empty. Just as they were about to give up for the night, a third officer, David Hunt appeared on the scene saying he had gotten a call about a strange object in the sky as well. Suddenly, the object that Norman had described appeared above the trees. It made a few passes over the three frightened men before flying off into the night.

The next day they found out that the same object was seen flying over Hampton, a town laying in the very direction they had seen the craft fly off to. Bertrand, an Air Force veteran, was quite vocal that he did not recognize the type of craft as being anything made by human hands.

BLIND

In November of 1997, two people were driving to Maine when they saw a crescent-shaped craft in the sky begin to hover directly in front of their car. When their vehicle approached the ship, it (much like in the Hill abduction) plummeted towards them at an impossible speed. The illumination thrown off by the craft seemed to increase as it fell until the occupants of the car were all but blind. Just as abruptly as their vision had left them, it returned. The craft, somehow, was gone. The two people exited the car and tried to see where the ship might have flown off to. But it was gone as if it had never existed.

THE STUFF OF NIGHTMARES

In 1998, over the course of several days, multiple witnesses called in reports of strange lights hovering in the sky near Hampton Beach. Many of these witnesses got photographs and video of the green lights which were shining brightly from a tadpole shaped aircraft of some kind.

Some of the people who called in the reports or took pictures said that later on in the evening they suffered from migraine headaches and had series of nightmares. The headaches and bad dreams seemed to crop up again each evening that the lights returned even if the witnesses didn't personally see the craft on those nights. When the lights stopped appearing over the ocean the headaches and nightmares also ended.

THE EYES HAVE IT

A North Hampton man awoke one night in 1999 to a bright light shining directly into his bedroom via a skylight above his bed. The light was a tight beam that was so carefully controlled that whomever was directing it was able to point it from a great distance directly into the man's right eye. When the man went to sit up, the beam of light retracted and he had a brief glimpse of a large oval-shaped ship of some kind speeding away through the trees.

Atypical Traditions

The Great Pumpkin Regatta

Goffstown has come up with an interesting annual fall festival. It begins with a weekend of dog costume contests, a barbeque, a flea market, and other events, and is capped off with an event that involves hollowing out enormous pumpkins and racing them down river.

There are plenty of pumpkin-related activities at Goffstown's annual Great Pumpkin Regatta. Many of them you would expect, like pumpkin pie eating contests and pumpkin carving contests.

There's also a weigh in with prizes for the biggest pumpkin. In 2000, Jim Beauchemin, the owner of one of these giant pumpkins, struck upon a novel idea concerning what to do with his giant pumpkin after the weigh in was done. Beauchemin hollowed out his gourd and floated it downriver—with himself inside to steer! The Great Pumpkin Regatta was born.

These giant pumpkins can range in weight from 600 to 1200 pounds, and when hollowed out, they are just big enough for one captain to man them. In the relatively short period of time since then, more and more vegetable boaters have gotten into the act, their wildly decorated pumpkin craft only outdone by the outrageous costumes their captains wear, with each trying to come up with better and better ways to steer their enormous orange boats.

While the race does draw quite a crowd of out-of-towners, this certainly isn't a sport just for tourists. It is normal for the boaters to include town selectmen and police officers, just as crazily dressed as the rest of the competition. This race is not just all fun and games. The Great Pumpkin Regatta raises funds each year for the Goffstown Main Street Program.

New Hampshire State Road Kill Auction

Eighty-five percent of New Hampshire is wooded, so it shouldn't be surprising that the state has a large number of wild woodland creatures roaming about. Or that sometimes these critters try crossing the state's highways at inopportune times. Motorists are welcome to take home any moose or deer they hit. If they choose not to and the highway department gets to the animal quickly, it's usually dressed and the meat donated. But what to do with all the things people don't normally eat? The foxes, beavers, opossums, squirrels, raccoons, coyotes, and the like?

The state has come upon a novel way to get rid of these animals and make a few bucks in the bargain. Over the course of the year, all the road kill picked up in the state is sent to the state-owned White Farm in Concord to be frozen. Once a year these frozen carcasses are brought out and put up on the auction block where hobbyist taxidermists, and who knows who else, battle it out for choice animals. The Fish and Game Department receives the profits and it is, all around, a good deal for everyone involved (minus the animals of course).

Much to the disappointment of taxidermy enthusiasts in New England, the Road Kill Auction has been put on hold in recent years due to an increase of rabies in the state.

PLACES

HAUNTED CEMETERIES

BEEBE CEMETERY

When Reverend George Beebe came to Star Island, the second largest island in the Isles of Shoals chain, in 1857, he never could have guessed that his name would still be associated with the place more than a hundred years later. At the time, the island seemed remote, even though it was located only six miles off the coast, and less than a hundred people lived on the island at any given time. During the 1800s the island had become a popular retreat for tuberculosis patients. As the number of sick visitors increased, the number of residents declined sharply. With a dwindling flock to tend to, Beebe turned his eye towards other works he could start up on the island to help fill his ever increasing amounts of free time.

Reverend Beebe began, among other things, the first cemetery on Star Island. Over a period of days, he cleared the land with his own hands and then waited to see the graveyard fill up with the faithful. But the tuberculosis patients who didn't recover tended to want their bodies shipped home for burial and the residents of Star Island were mostly fisherman who tended to die out at sea, no burial needed.

It is doubtful that when the project was begun that Reverend Beebe would have ever expected to see his own family name in the cemetery he had created. But, in 1863, the Reverend's entire family would fall ill with consumption, as tuberculosis was called at the time. Three of the Reverend's young daughters would die, becoming not only the first people to be interred at the cemetery their father had built, but also the only people to ever be buried there.

Heart broken over the loss of his girls Reverend Beebe and his remaining family left Star Island. The population on the island continued to dwindle. In time a grand hotel, the Oceanic, would be built here. It thrived for awhile, as did the two or three other large hotels dotting some of the other Isles of Shoals, but eventually the great hotels in New Hampshire's mountains won out as the most popular tourists destinations in the state. The Oceanic would sit empty for a number of years, all but forgotten in its odd little corner of the world. Ultimately, the grand hotel would become a conference center and religious retreat, which it is still used for today. In 1915, the hotel, all the outbuildings, even the entire island, were purchased by the Star Island Corporation. Star Island ceased to have full-time residents and the island is now a more or less self-sufficient town run by the corporation for the sake of the religious conferences held at the Oceanic.

While most of the hotel grounds are beautifully landscaped and carefully maintained, large portions of the island are left in a more natural state. One of these natural spaces completely covered the Beebe Cemetery until recent years. The cemetery had been hidden, totally forgotten and completely covered by New Hampshire wild flowers and tall grass for close to a hundred years. But that does not mean that the Beebe girls were as easily forgotten. Many hotel visitors over the years reported seeing the ghostly figure of a small child dashing through the trees or were surprised by childish laughter while walking the hotel grounds. A few heard an older girl's voice reading Bible verses and assumed it was someone else at a religious conference with them until they looked around and realized they were all alone. The ghosts were a mystery until the small cemetery was finally uncovered. Once the weeds were cleared away, three small headstones were found.

Millie Beebe's reads "Dying she kneeled down and prayed: Jesus, take me up to the lighted place. And he did" Her older sister, only seven when she died, Mitty's says simply, "I don't want to die, but I'll do just as Jesus wants me to" The third tombstone is, after well over one hundred years near the sea, unreadable.

The Beebe Family cemetery has since been cleared of the obscuring trees and weeds and since the upkeep on the land has continued, signs of ghostly activity have tapered off some.

There are other creatures of some kind who have been said to roam the island at night. Many people have been awakened by a scratching noise at their windows as though something was trying desperately to get inside. Other times people hear soft indecipherable whispering accompanying the scratching sounds. Some, since the Beebe Cemetery was found, have chalked the occurrence up to the ghosts of the young sisters. But historical evidence shows that the noise has been reported since long before the Beebe family ever set foot on Star Island.

Chillingly, many early accounts of the phenomena claim it was caused by vampires. The belief in these undead creatures of the night was quite widespread in the early part of the history of the United States, and is deeply rooted in the folk beliefs of New England. Historically, tuberculosis was often misdiagnosed as "proof" of vampire visitations so it should, perhaps, not come as a surprise that an island popular as a tuberculosis retreat was also thought to be a hunting ground for vampires.

VALE END AND LAUREL HILL CEMETERIES

Vale End Cemetery in Wilton is a notable one. Firstly because, you guessed it, it's haunted. But the really unusual thing about this cemetery is that it's haunted by a column of blue light.

The tall column of light emanates from the grave of Mary Ritter in the northeast corner of Vale End Cemetery. The light is most common in the spring and fall, particularly during foggy nights. Because the light has only been seen at Ritter's grave, it has been assumed that this is her spirit, even if it's chosen to show itself in this strange way. This has garnered Mary Ritter the posthumous nickname the "Blue Lady."

Whether the light is Mary Ritter's ghost, or something stranger, is debatable. But the Blue Lady of Vale End is in good ghostly company. Several other spirits call this cemetery home. Native American spirits have been seen and sensed in and around the graves leading to speculation that, long before the town of Wilton existed, the ground that Vale End sits upon was a burial ground for the areas first inhabitants. These spirits have been described as protective forces that scare away vandals or others who they feel are disrespecting this hallowed ground. They are said to be particularly vindictive forces against anyone who removes items, even those of no known value, sentimental or otherwise, from the cemetery.

Other Vale End ghosts include a small boy (possibly one of Mary Ritter's children, as she was a mother of seven), an old General and *his* daughter, a young man from the 1800s who committed suicide and is buried just outside the cemetery walls, and even the spirit of a black and white dog.

The dog has been seen as a dark grey cloud of energy, passing through people and graves as if it doesn't see them. Audio recordings taken when this dark cloud has been seen record the dog barking, happily it seems, even though no dogs were heard at the time the recordings were taken.

As strange as a ghostly dog might seem, it is definitely Vale End's Blue Lady that captures the most attention, if only for being a more unusual visual haunting than most people are used to. But Vale End can't claim to have the only "light" ghost in New Hampshire. The Blue Lady can't even claim the title of the only light ghost in Wilton! Laurel Hill Cemetery has an equally laser like ghost that appears in photographs as a bright purple streak. This odd purple light has appeared in all sections of the cemetery and is sometimes accompanied by the spirit of a young man clad in an outfit that was all the rage back in the early 1800s.

VALLEY STREET CEMETERY

Ann carefully adjusted the lens on her camera, trying to get a close up shot of the scrollwork on the top of the tombstone in front of her. The camera was new; she cursed herself silently as she fumbled with the unfamiliar buttons along the top, trying to get the shot she needed to complete her photo project for school. On the screen of the digital camera, just as she clicked the button to take her photo, she saw a woman walk into the frame.

· "Excuse me," Ann snapped, irritated. "I'm trying to take a picture."

But her complaint trailed off to nothing as she glanced up from the camera to look at the person she was talking to. That's because there was no one near the tombstone. Confused, Ann looked all around her, but as far as she could see, the cemetery

In early 2006 a photographer had what she thinks was a ghostly encounter near these three historic graves.

was empty. It made no sense; Ann had been so sure she had seen a woman dart into the picture and stand behind the grave marker. Feeling a sudden chill, Ann hit the review option on her camera and started to page through the photos she had taken that day. In the final photograph, the one she was so sure had been ruined by a careless pedestrian, there was no figure to be found . . . though the tombstone she had been trying to capture seemed to have a strange cloud of very thin fog around it.

The encounter Ann experienced might seem strange . . . anywhere other than Valley Street Cemetery in Manchester. This twenty-acre graveyard is the largest green space in the city of Manchester, it's listed on the National Registry of Historic Places, is considered a classic example of a traditional New England garden-style cemetery, and has become a well-known ghost hotspot in the state of New Hampshire.

First built in 1841, the carefully landscaped cemetery quickly became the final resting spot for many of New Hampshire's rich and famous residents. The cemetery hosts, among many others, two New Hampshire governors, sixty Civil War soldiers, a handful of veterans from the Revolutionary War, at least one fighter hailing from the French and Indian War, scores of former Manchester mayors, as well as the descendants of the city's first founding families. However, the northwest section of the cemetery was set aside for the paupers of Manchester, poor residents or homeless transients who could

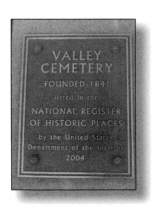

Valley Street Cemetery was added to the National Registry of Historic Places in 2004.

not afford a "proper" burial were interred here with little regard or fanfare. But even that is better then what faced some of the dead who call this cemetery home. Shortly after the opening of the celebrated garden cemetery, Manchester faced a series of cholera outbreaks and the victims of this dreaded disease were placed in mass graves in the northeastern section of the cemetery, without even gravestones to mark their deaths.

One of the Valley Cemetery mausoleums. Each one is unique and some are uniquely haunted.

Not surprisingly, both these sections of Valley Street Cemetery are known for their ghosts. Many people walking through these parts of Valley Street Cemetery have experienced roving cold spots on even the warmest of days. Others are plagued by faintly heard murmurings they can find no source for. The sounds are said to be faint, though inexplicable, and tinged with an unaccountable sadness. Some people who hear this sound report feeling as though they were being led by unseen hands griping their shoulders. It is not impossible to imagine that some long ago cholera victim, without even a name or date on a tombstone to comfort them, is trying desperately to reach out and be recognized in some way.

However, if these ghosts were the extent of Valley Street Cemetery's paranormal occurrences, they would barely be worth mentioning. Those ghosts are sad, though not particularly scary, and are easy to ignore . . . especially for people who deny the existence of ghosts in the first place. But Valley Street Cemetery has several more outgoing spirits and a few downright frightful ones. There are thirteen (yes, lucky thirteen) mausoleums dotting the grounds, each with its own unique architectural style and atmosphere. One of these, the Frederick Smyth mausoleum, sports Grecian pillars, white marble construction, and seems to be the center of two opposing ghostly forces.

A young woman, who is said to smell of old-fashioned floral perfume, is the one most often sensed lingering around the Smyth mausoleum. Visitors who encounter her often describe feeling that she wants them to leave the area and that she is very protective, of both the area around the mausoleum and of themselves. And visitors to this part of the cemetery may just need her protection. The second ghost who haunts this mausoleum is an angry older man who carries a cloud of tense negative feelings around with him that even some of the most psychically numb visitors have reported sensing. He is proceeded by a blast of frigid air and has even been accused of cracking or damaging tombstones nearby the Smyth mausoleum.

It is unclear who these two spirits were in life or if they even knew each other while alive. Ghost Quest, a New Hampshire ghost

The back of the Smyth mausoleum. The front faces a shear thirty-foot drop overlooking the valley that gave this cemetery its name.

hunting group, made several trips to Valley Street Cemetery to try and answer some of these questions and once got the ghost hunting experience of a lifetime. While walking through the grounds, Raven Duclos, a psychic, felt drawn to the mausoleum. As she walked around the building she felt waves of melancholy emanating from the tomb. Just as she reached the doorway she heard a woman's voice screaming at her to get away quickly. No one else in the group heard the voice, but when they returned to the office and played back their audio recording, a standard piece of ghost hunting equipment, had captured the sound clearly.

Valley Street Cemetery has changed a lot since it was started in the 1840s. It fell into decline during more recent times and it is sometimes hard to picture it as it must have been in its heyday, dotted with almost as many gazebos as gravestones, with a picturesque stream running through the center, and ornate horse-drawn carriages pulling gaily dressed Manchester residents along the cobblestone paths. Time and vandals have taken more of a toll on the cemetery than the ghosts ever will. Since 2002, a dedicated group of residents have been working to restore the cemetery to its former glory. They have managed to remove much of the graffiti that has marred the thirteen mausoleums and they have saved nearly 400 historic trees. It was with the onset of the restoration work that the ghostly activity in the cemetery seemed to ramp up to newfound proportions, though it is impossible to say if the ghosts became more active or if there were just more living people there to encounter them.

Blood Cemetery

Ask even the most casual ghost hunting aficionado what's the most haunted cemetery in New Hampshire and more than likely the first place they mention will be Blood Cemetery. But you won't find Blood Cemetery on any map; that's just the name locals call Pine Hill Cemetery in Hollis.

The Blood moniker isn't an affectation someone thought up because it sounded spooky. It is thanks to Abel Blood, one of several Blood family members to be buried in this graveyard, and the main character in most of the ghost stories you'll hear about Pine Hill. Most notable among the Blood Cemetery lore is that Abel's headstone changes at night. The tombstone's most noticeable feature is a hand, finger outstretched pointing up towards Heaven. This was common enough graveyard iconography in Abel's day and wouldn't be worth mentioning at all if the hand always stayed in place. Locals swear that at night the upwards pointing finger instead points down. This has sparked many different legends about secret occult practices and black masses said to have been held by Abel during his lifetime, or perhaps even by the entire Blood clan. However, the only evidence for this is the tombstone. In life, by all accounts that survive today, Abel and his forefathers were hardworking Christians, good to their neighbors and important figures in the town and in their church.

Another pervasive legend is that Abel's ghost haunts Pine Hill Cemetery because he was murdered and his spirit is confused and troubled. Abel, it is said, roams the cemetery trying to find his grave and that of his wife, who died shortly after giving birth

The Aretas Blood Family Tomb under construction in 2007.

The main gates to the cemetery were replaced as part of the conservation effort to bring back Manchester's famous "garden cemetery."

"The Chapel" is another unique building in this haunted cemetery. Built in 1932, this English Gothic-style chapel has fallen into disrepair and is closed to the public. It sits very close to the haunted Smyth mausoleum.

to their one child. The only problem with this story is that Abel wasn't murdered. He lived well into his seventies, not too shabby for the 1800s.

Pine Hill is an old cemetery. Many of the graves are so old that their tombstones have not survived and the graves lie unmarked. Cemetery records tell us that close to 300 people have been buried here. Considering how many people have become permanent residents of Pine Hill, it should come as no surprise that Abel is not the only one of them who is thought to be restless. Visitors have heard ghostly murmurings and warnings, have been pursued by cold spots, and have even felt as if something unseen was leading them around the grounds. There is at least one ghost at Pine Hill who manifests itself by olfactory means. This spirit is known for a spicy scent that some have compared to Old Spice aftershave. Many people have reported sensing some kind of angry presence in the cemetery or seeing a lone dark shape floating through the graves at dusk.

This graveyard is a well-known spot for taking ghost photographs or trying to record EVPs. A quick Google search online will turn up dozens of websites that have orb photographs that were taken at the cemetery. When most people think of "ghost photography" they imagine a picture of a wispy, near transparent, woman in old-fashioned clothes floating several feet from the ground, preferably set against a background of some obviously abandoned old wreck of a house. But full-bodied apparitions like these are extremely, extremely rare—and it is even more unlikely that one would capture the image of one on film.

The absolutely most common type of ghost photography is a picture showing "orbs." Orbs can take the shape of small fuzzy-edged dots, in a plethora of colors, or even as bright streaks of lights in varying color. Many people have taken orb photographs and not even realized it, passing the anomaly off as dust on the lens when they look at their pictures (on the other hand, a lot of would-be ghost hunters are convinced they've taken orb photographs when really all they did was take a picture of some dust on their camera lens). Many people pass all orb photographs off as explainable phenomena. Others believe that these photos are proof of life after death, in some form. Even within the paranormal community there is much debate about what orbs mean. To some they are simply a type of energy showing there is some kind of otherworldly activity going on nearby. Others believe they are a type of ghost in and of themselves. No matter what you believe it is undeniable that, for some reason, photographers get more orb photographs in Pine Hill Cemetery than most other places.

Blood Cemetery is so haunted that even the road leading to it is plagued with paranormal encounters. Many people driving up Pine Hill Road have been alarmed to see a young child run out of the woods towards their car, flagging them down frantically. Local legend is that the boy lived on this road in life and that his family was murdered one night. Now the boy's spirit spends most nights still trying to flag down help for his poor family. Legend doesn't give us a name or time for the boy, and records don't turn up any reports that are likely linked to him, so it seems unlikely that he is really a long ago murder victim. Who the boy is, and why he is in such desperate need of help, remains a mystery.

POINT OF GRAVES

Point of Graves Burial Ground in Portsmouth dates from the 1600s and some of the earliest gravestones in the state can be seen here today. The land for this burial ground was donated by Captain John Pickering, although he continued to use it as grazing land for his prized cows even after the first bodies began to be buried there!

The Pickering family used the land as a burial spot long before bequeathing it to the city of Portsmouth so there is no way of telling just how many people are buried there today or how old some of

This plaque at the entrance to Point of Graves Burial Ground directs visitors to the more famous of the cemetery's residents.

those graves may be. Despite the age of this cemetery, today, it is well maintained and draws visitors from all over the state who come to see the tombstones carved by notable stonecutters of days gone by or to view the graves of some prominent New Hampshirites.

Like many old cemeteries, this one seems to be a haven for ghosts and odd occurrences. Many people are stalked by footsteps that have no known earthly source. Many visitors seem to be

Above and following:
Point of Graves is visited as much for its beautiful gravestones as for its ghosts.

particularly plagued by small shoves and pulls at their clothing as they walk away from the 1717 grave of Elizabeth Pierce. The sensations never happens to people approaching the grave, and instead, seem to be caused by something unseen that is trying to get them to stay.

Visitors with cameras, or this day and age camera phones, oftentimes get an uncanny souvenir of their visit. The Vaughan tomb is the center of these photographic excursions. Though no ghosts have been seen there, the simple rectangular gravestone sometimes appears in photographs surrounded by a peculiar greenish-yellow glow. To date, no one has been able to come up with a sound scientific reason for the strange aura that encompasses this gravestone. Skeptics say that the glow is just the reflection of a nearby street light on the smooth white stone of the crypt. But is should be said that the glow is visible no matter which angle or side of the grave you look at. More importantly, the Vaughan tomb it is the only grave to glow in such a way. If it truly was just the reflection of an outside light source, wouldn't the graves surrounding it glow as well?

   In probably the single most unusual occurrence happening at any New Hampshire cemetery, one day a group of tourists on a ghost walking tour, accompanied by a reporter who would later publish an article about what he experienced, got more than just

The Vaughan tomb may not be as intricately inscripted as some of the other gravestones at Point of Graves, but it is the most haunted.

a quick haunted history lesson. As the day slid into evening and the sky above Point of Graves Burial Ground tuned black, the clouds above the cemetery were said to roil and turn wispy pink. The fifteen witnesses all agreed that the clouds clearly formed the bodies and wings of singing angels.

THE MYSTERY OF MYSTERY HILL: AMERICA'S STONEHENGE

Mystery Hill is just one small ridge in a larger, and equally mysterious, plot of land that is known today as America's Stonehenge. Altogether this popular outdoor museum and tourist attraction is comprised of thirty acres and the snow shoe trails that can be accessed from this spot travel through more than a hundred acres. Mystery Hill itself features a series of stone monoliths; the rest of the complex is covered in meandering stone walls and other strange stone creations. There is as much debate and controversy

over this site as there are tall tales, outlandish claims, and flat out wild theories.

In the early 1700 and 1800s, this land was owned by a succession of first-born sons of the Pattee family, eventually falling into the hands of Jonathan Pattee, a farmer. The land had been falling in and out of their family's hands for years, with Pattees moving and leaving seemingly every other generation. When Jonathan became owner of the land, the odd stone structures didn't phase him in the least. He built his home and outbuildings all but intertwined with the already existing stone sculptures and didn't seem to give them much thought beyond that. Pattee would live on the land for thirty years before striking out for someplace new after his home burnt to the ground. He was something of an enigmatic (okay, eccentric) figure himself and many people, upon seeing the stone monoliths for the first time, assumed he had built them himself for reasons no one could fathom. Locals began calling the former farm Pattee's Caves.

In the 1930s, Pattee's Caves were bought by an insurance salesman named William Goodwin. Goodwin, realizing there was something more going on then could be passed off as the creation of a New Hampshire farmer, renamed the spot Mystery Hill and began to market it as a tourist attraction. This was not simply greed on the part of Goodwin. He was something of an archaeological hobbyist. Originally believing Mystery Hill to be a Viking settlement of some kind, he eventually decided that Mystery Hill was actually the ruins of a monastery of Culdee Monks that pre-dated Columbus's discovery of North America. The Culdees were a religious order, dating from the Middle Ages, that were found in what is now Scotland, Ireland, and Britain. The Culdee's were targeted by Viking persecution and they eventually fled to Iceland. Goodwin was sure that the Culdees must have continued their travels, finally ending up in what is now New England—discovering and settling the land long before the Vikings or Christopher Columbus. If Goodwin could prove his theory, one which is still

Dozens of these small stone cave-like structures dot the area once known as Mystery Hill.

hotly debated today, it would make his name in archaeological circles and make him highly sought after to theologians, who would be interested in the remains of the religious sect as it was considered to be absolutely free of any Roman influence on the Christian religion.

Almost as soon as Goodwin bought the property, he started publicizing his theory. A slew of articles announcing that the Irish were the original settlers of the North American continent started coming out in New England newspapers. Some articles described the Mystery Hill site as a stone village. Others, because of a large slab of stone Goodwin named a sacrificial altar, promoted the idea of it being the site of religious sacrifices. One article described the sacrificial altar as being the site of numerous religious murders . . . or possibly just a grape press used to make wine.

The problem with all of this media attention was, of course, that no true fieldwork had been done at the Mystery Hill site and that Goodwin had no proof of anything other than that of the most circumstantial kind to back up his claims. The media of the time didn't seem worried about any of that. This may have resulted in larger crowds paying the admission fee at Mystery Hill, but it stood in the way of any serious archaeological work being done at the site. It was not until 1939 that a journalist by the name of Hugh Hencken began to publicly dispute Goodwin's Irish settlement theory. Goodwin became increasingly distraught as Hencken published more and more in a series of articles pointing out flaws in the Irish settlement theory. Slowly other publications also began to point out problems with the amateur archaeologists theory.

It was not until 1950, when William Goodwin died, that serious archaeological work began to take place at Mystery Hill and the first

Some of the stones used to create these structures weigh several tons and it is unclear how they were made or for what purpose.

radiocarbon dating tests were done. Ultimately the site would be renamed "America's Stonehenge" to further disassociate it with Goodwin's now more or less quite ridiculed theories.

Scientific study has done little to untangle the true story behind Mystery Hill. In life William Goodwin moved many of the stones out of their original position in a desperate attempt to create proof to support his theory. Even before Goodwin's time, many of the stones were dug up and carted away to build bridges and other public works projects across New Hampshire and Massachusetts. Shackles have been found in some of the underground caves that have led people to the conclusion that the Pattee family was a long line of abolitionists and that they used their land as a major stop on the Underground Railroad, but carbon dating has shown that many of the structures pre-date this period of history. Some of the stones bear inscriptions that have been likened to several various ancient writing systems. Still others indicate that the stone structures now seem to be very common farming implements used in the 1700s. But it is hard to say if that was their original purpose or if the Pattee family merely appropriated already existing structures for these purposes. Specifically the stone monoliths atop Mystery Hill

Many people feel that the names William Goodwin gave to many of the stone structures, such as the "sacrificial table," have held back serious scientific research at America's Stonehenge.

On top of the stone structures and miles of rock walls, America's Stonehenge is a perfectly aligned astronomical calendar, just like its namesake in England. Pointed stones, such as this one, mark sunrises and sunsets on specific dates throughout the year.

One of the hiking trails at America's Stonehenge follows the calendar stones around the property.

have been said to be an astrologically aligned calendar, but again, it is debatable if they were the creation of a pre-Columbian, non-Native American, culture or a creation of someone more modern for their own purposes.

Today America's Stonehenge is still open to the public. It has been expanded from being solely an archaeological tourist attraction to an alpaca farm and snow shoe trails. On sunsets and sunrises on the days of equinox and solstice events are held near the pointed stones marking that day on the astronomical calendar.

CHURCH OF THE STIGMATA

According to a recent Gallup poll, New Hampshire is tied with its neighbor to the west, Vermont, for having the lowest church attendance in the United States. That's why it's so ironic that one of the Holiest experiences one can imagine is said to have taken place in St. Joseph Church in Berlin, New Hampshire on June 1, 2000.

There were many witnesses in the church that day who saw a red, blood-like substance running down the walls along either side of a statue of Saint Joseph. One member grabbed a nearby ladder and decided to take a closer look. From this vantage, it was discovered that the substance was running wetly down from the forty-year-old statue of Jesus on the cross hanging directly above the altar and statue of St. Joseph.

Word spread quickly, first from person to person, then to the media, that a vision of the stigmata had occurred in Berlin. Within days, hundreds of people were lined up to see the inside of the church where the miracle was said to have occurred. They found, tacked to the front door, a lengthy letter from the priest at St. Joseph. Father Roberge's note stressed, repeatedly, that the stigmata had never happened, that absolutely nothing out of the ordinary had happened, and that the substance had been brought to a local hospital laboratory and had definitely not been blood of any kind.

The people who were there that day swore up and down they had seen something extraordinary and refused to back down. The church likewise held fast to their stance. In time, the crowds of hundred dwindled back to their normal attendance numbers.

COVERED BRIDGE HOUSE

When is a bridge not a bridge? It may sound like the beginning of a joke but if so, the punch line can be found in Webster. So, when is a bridge not a bridge? When it's a house.

In 1909, Webster condemned the covered bridge that had spanned the Blackwater River for years. Most often in these cases, the bridge would have been demolished by the town or left to rot over the river, either way the bridge would be gone and good riddance to it. Then Jessie Pearson got involved. Jessie bought the bridge, had workman take it apart, moved it a few miles away, and then instructed the workman to rebuild it precisely the way it was when they tore it down.

Once rebuilt on her own land, Jessie had both ends capped off and started to live in the building. Over the years, she added a loft, a fieldstone fireplace along one wall, and wrapped a balcony partially around the outside. The result is a somewhat drafty, though definitely one-of-a-kind, dwelling.

When Jessie died, the house was passed on to her brother, who promptly sold the thing. He never would have guessed it at the time, but years later, his own son, Jessie's nephew Jon, would buy the building back. He lives there today, with every intent of keeping the covered bridge house his aunt created in the family for years to come.

Lost Tourist Attractions

Much of New Hampshire's tourism centers around the great outdoors. In the summer, people flock to the state's lake regions for boating, swimming, fishing, and water sports. In the winter the White Mountains are a popular destination for skiers and snowboarders. Amusement parks like Storyland, with more than fifty years under its belt, Clarks Trading Post, with over eighty, or Canobie Lake Park, which can claim over a hundred years in operation, have been around for generations for families to enjoy. More recent additions to New Hampshire's tourism roster include the water park Liquid Planet, in Candia.

But, as the old saying goes, nothing lasts forever. It's as true for tourists spots as it is for anything else. And, with tourism such a big part of the state, it shouldn't be a surprise to anyone that some tourist attractions have faded, changed, or been forgotten over the years. Many of these lost attractions make perfect sense. For instance, when skiing first became a popular draw in the White Mountains, every farmer with a slight elevation and the ingenuity to set up a rope tow of some sort was quick to market their snow-covered fields as a ski resort—oftentimes to the disappointment of the thrifty skier who was trying to save a few bucks by avoiding the larger resorts. Other attractions rise and fall in popularity for different reasons.

THE MUMMIES OF WOODSTOCK

Yes, New Hampshire has a town called Woodstock. No, it's not *that* Woodstock; that's in New York. And the iconic 1969 music festival took place in Bethel anyway. But that's all beside the point. The important thing about the New Hampshire Woodstock is that, once upon a time, it boasted an attraction called The Mummies.

This attraction is actually a naturally occurring bit of river erosion along the side of Crooked Brook. The water, for whatever reason, has worn down the bedrock in a unique way that does make it appear as though along the side of the river a line of shrouded bodies are laid out in a row, one right next to the other.

In the 1920s, thanks to the spectacular discovery of King Tutankhamen's tomb in Egypt and the subsequent world-wide tour of his artifacts, America went a little Egypt crazy. New Hampshire was no different than anywhere else. Even today you'll find a fun retro-Egypt decorating theme in the carefully restored Capital Center for the Arts in Concord. No doubt "the Mummies" attraction in Woodstock was named around the same time to capitalize on the time periods fascination with everything Egyptian. The softly rounded ridges are a unique enough phenomenon but one can't help but feel that the name must have seemed at least a little misleading to anyone who went out of their way to view New Hampshire's "mummies." One does have to wonder how much the name might have helped kill the site as an attraction. There must have been more than just one sad-faced little kid who made the trek to Woodstock to see the mummies and was disappointed to find it was some bumpy bedrock.

The mummies do still exist today, though they are no longer an attraction. In fact, the only way to get to them is to cut across some privately owned property, which could earn you a vacation in one of New Hampshire's prisons, or at least a hefty fine.

Rock Rimmon

Almost every town in New Hampshire has a stone crag somewhere in their area looking vaguely like a face that they would like to see replace the famed "Old Man in the Mountain." Mount Pemigewasset has their Indian Head Profile. Marlow has a similar outcropping of stone on Bald Hill. Pawtuckaway State Park in Nottingham has an entire collection of vaguely Easter Island-ish stone faces in Boulder Field. For that matter

Rock Rimmon Park, at the base of the stone, would have been one of the biggest tourist draws in the state, if the stone profile had not mysteriously disappeared.

Manchester's Rock Rimmon was once the site of a rock profile much like the famous Old Man in the Mountain.

both Moultonborough and New Boston have stones famous for being frog shaped. So what makes the stone face in Manchester so different? The profile seen on Rock Rimmon takes its place among the weird and unexplainable because one day, before it could even become a tourist attraction, the face on Rock Rimmon completely disappeared.

In 1925, the State Forestry Commissioner, John Corliss, discovered the very distinct face of a Native American naturally built into Rock Rimmon. The face was said to be even easier to see then the famous Old Man in the Mountain, and it caused quite a stir that no one had ever noticed it before when the news hit the local papers. The story was published in several newspapers around the state along with photos of the Old Man of Rimmon Rock. The face was photographed many times and was plain to see from a certain spot in Rimmon Park. Manchester's parks commission began plans to build viewing platforms and advertising hoping that their Old Man would draw away visitors from up north and bring them into Manchester. Without warning, or explanation, all the plans were dropped. Stranger still, no one could seem to find the face anymore!

No rock slides were reported, and the noise from the collapse surely would have drawn the attention of local residents, if nothing else. Although photos of the naturally occurring formation survive, the exact location you needed to stand at in order to see it has been obscured by time. No one has seen it since.

THE OLD MAN IN THE MOUNTAIN

Call him the Great Stone Face, the Profile, or his most famous moniker: The Old Man in the Mountain. Or for that matter you could call him the Greatest Lost Tourist Attraction of Them All. Call him anything at this point. The name doesn't matter much considering that now he's gone.

The profile of the Old Man in the Mountain, located in Franconia Notch, graces New Hampshire road signs, the New Hampshire state quarter, postage stamps, and tourist trinkets galore. Just about the only place you can't see the collection of five ledges and cliffs that made up his great craggy face is on Cannon Mountain where tourists since the 1800s have come from all over to view him. That's because he collapsed on May 3, 2003.

Many attempts have been made by groups, headed for the most part by local businesses that have seen a sharp decline in tourism dollars since the Old Man collapsed, to rebuild the stone face. But many people feel that a reproduction Old Man is worthless. This is somewhat ironic. What many people don't realize is that the Old Man profile was not one hundred percent naturally occurring to begin with and that it had been propped up for most of the past hundred years to help it keep it's face like shape.

A year after the rock slide that demolished the profile, the state revealed a row of coin operated viewfinders that, for a small price, show how the mountain used to look with the face still on it. Needless to say, the businesses that depend on the tourist trade find these to be a poor substitute. Within the past few years an Old Man Memorial was designed and decided upon, although it has run into some funding issues.

It is an odd end for a tourist attraction that has been the official New Hampshire state emblem since 1945 and of which Daniel Webster once said: "Men hang out their signs indicative of their respective trades; shoe makers hang out a gigantic shoe; jewelers a monster watch, and the dentist hangs out a gold tooth; but up in the Mountains of New Hampshire, God Almighty has hung out a sign to show that there He makes men."

THE WORST WEATHER ON EARTH

Since Mount Washington, located in New Hampshire's Presidential mountain range, sits at the convergence of three storm tracks, it would be an understatement to call the weather atop the mountain erratic. In fact, Mount Washington has been called the home of the worst weather on Earth. It is common for snow to fall at any time of the year on the summit. Mount Washington holds the record for the fastest ever recorded surface wind speed, a hair raising 231 miles per hour, and wind speeds exceeding those of hurricane force are found on the summit about 110 days out of every year.

Long before it earned the title of being home to the worst weather on Earth for its record-breaking wind speeds, Mount Washington was known to the Natives that preceded the white settlers as Agiocochook, "the home of the Great Spirit." And it *is* a great spirit of sorts, the highest point in the state and third highest on the Eastern coast. This has made it a premier destination for glider flying and, in honor of its significant presence to this sport, it has been named as one of very few National Landmarks of Soaring. At the summit you can also find the Mount Washington Weather Observatory, which has been making weather observations since 1870, making it the first of its kind in the world.

It is a draw for residents and tourists alike. There are several ways to top Mount Washington and experience its sub-arctic climate for yourself. The Mount Washington Auto Road offers anyone with a car the opportunity to drive to the top (check your brakes before you go!) and the Cog Railway has been operating since the mid 1800s. Outdoorsy types can, of course, hike their way to the top. Mount Washington is part of the Appalachian Trail and is extremely popular to what are known as thru-hikers. Thru-hikers aren't on the trail for just a day or two, and they aren't just aiming to reach the top of a particular mountain before starting their way home. Thru-hikers are in it for the long haul, going the entirety of the trail before calling it quits.

To assist the thru-hikers, and to help curb the deaths that sometimes occur on Mount Washington due to inexperienced and ill-prepared hikers, there are a series of Alps-style lodging along the trail known as the high huts. All in all there are eight high huts to be found in the White Mountains, all under the care of the Appalachian Mountain Club. Each one is roughly a days hike away from the next and they offer a place to sleep, a place to cook some food (or during the summer to have dinner or breakfast served to you), and a chance to tell tale tales with your fellow hikers.

Not one, not two, not even three of the high huts are said to be haunted—all eight are! And, fittingly enough, the high hut atop the tallest mountain is said to be the most haunted.

The Lakes of the Clouds Hut on Mount Washington can be found at about 5,372 feet, roughly a mile below the summit, making it the highest of all the huts. It is also the largest and the busiest, as can be told by the snarky nickname veteran hikers know it by—the Lakes of the *Crowds*. Some of those crowding the Lakes of Clouds Hut are supernatural in nature.

Those familiar with the scariest of the Lakes of Clouds ghosts call it the Presence. The Presence usually shows itself as a dark, glowing figure. It wanders around the dining room of the hut, or just outside it, tapping on windows. One Appalachian Mountain Club volunteer had a much more frightening experience though.

He had been sent up alone to the Lakes of Clouds to decide what needed to be done to prepare the hut for the upcoming busy season. Winter had just ended and damage needed to be assessed and shelves restocked with necessaries. When he didn't return after a few hours, people started to worry. When he didn't answer any calls on the walkie talkie they got really worried. After a day had passed several other volunteers decided to hike up and check on him.

Inside the hut everything looked normal. They could tell he had made it there fine and nothing seemed out of place except for the fact that they couldn't find their co-worker. Finally, a small noise coming from inside a kitchen cabinet alerted them.

They found the missing AMC member wedged underneath, soaked with sweat, and positively terrified. He refused to speak about his experience until they helped him make his way down the mountain, and away from the Lakes of Clouds Hut, as quickly as possible.

He said that things had felt wrong from the moment he had entered the hut the day before. He couldn't shake the feeling that he was not alone and more than once he felt a presence approach him from behind. One of these times he turned quickly, hoping to catch someone playing a prank on him; instead, he saw a demonic face pressed up against the glass of a nearby window glaring at him—something that should have been impossible since the window was boarded up from the outside. As he watched each window in the room, all were boarded up as the first one, and all were filled with precisely the same evil face.

There are at least two other ghosts at the Lakes of Clouds hut. They are said to belong to two New Yorkers who lost their lives on Mount Washington in 1900. That year, William Curtis and Alan Ormsbec were caught in an ice storm in mid-summer. Both men tried valiantly to find shelter but died in the process. A year later, the Lakes of Clouds hut would open at the spot where they had died. It was too late to help Curtis and Ormsbec, but it would keep other hikers from meeting the same fate.

Almost immediately after the hut opened, a large plaque commemorating the spot where Curtis's body had been recovered was found pushed up against the door of the lodge instead of attached to a rock several yards away as it should have been. Not much was thought of it and the plaque was re-attached to the rock. Again it was found against the door, in precisely the same spot as before. This went on many, many times. No one ever saw the plaque in motion and it was never found anywhere except pressed against the door into the hut. Eventually, it was moved inside the hut and there is has remained ever since.

But beware, hikers who have made rude comments about the men who lost their lives on Mount Washington have reported being abused by an unseen force. Sharp slaps or punches to the chest by hands they cannot see seem to be this ghosts response to anyone who gets a little too full of themselves while climbing Mount Washington.

Castles in the Clouds

Lucknow

Just about everyone has heard of William Hearst, the famed newspaperman who was said to be the inspiration for Orson Welles classic 1941 film *Citizen Kane*. Today, Hearst is as famous for his outlandish Hearst Castle, the mansion he had built in the California hills, as for anything else he may have done in life. The William Hearst Castle is one of California's leading tourist attractions.

What few people know is that New Hampshire has their own version of William Hearst and his elaborate mansion—all because of a man named Thomas Plant.

Thomas Plant made his fortune thanks to patents on shoe making machinery, not newspaper publishing like Hearst, but this seemingly simple invention garnered the man riches that are staggering even by today's standards. Around 1913, a large chunk of this wealth went towards the purchase of a large tract of land on the top of Ossipee Mountain. All told, Plant would eventually come to own more than 6,000 acres atop the mountain, most of it with an astounding view of Lake Winnipesaukee and the surrounding mountains. Plant had the top of the mountain leveled, brought in over 1,000 Italian stone masons, and had them use the resulting rubble to build his fabulous mansion, many outbuildings, and miles upon miles of stone walls around it all. Working at a furious pace the entire enterprise was completed in just over three years.

The house was called Plant's Folly by everyone except for Mr. Plant and his wife. They christened the estate "Lucknow," possibly after a poem written by Mrs. Plant. However, like Hearst, Plant's luck didn't last. After spending enormous sums of money to build the home of his dreams, he, under advice from none other than Theodore Roosevelt, invested heavily in Russian currency. Soon afterwards, the Bolsheviks took down the Russian Czar, making the Russian currency worthless. Plant clung desperately to Lucknow, fighting foreclosure for most of his life. It was not simple fear that he would lose his dream home. More than anything, Plant feared the estate would be razed, turned into a gaudy hotel, or that the surrounding land would be sold off piecemeal and a tacky development spring up. Thomas Plant would die on July 11, 1941, just three short days after he received notice that his dream home was going to be sold at auction to the highest bidder.

The estate is still around today, now known by the name of "The Castle in the Clouds" as opposed to Lucknow or Plant's Folly. It is managed by the Lakes Region Conservation Trust and is open each and every day to the public during the spring and summer months. Plant's lavish home now has forty-five miles of hiking trails and is also available for functions and events.

KIMBALL CASTLE

Believe it or not there is a second castle overlooking Lake Winnipesaukee. This castle was also the creation of an eccentric and fabulously wealthy man, a railroad man by the name of Benjamin Ames Kimball. In 1897, Kimball bought a large tract of land on top of Locke's Hill in Gilford. Inspired by a German castle he had seen along the banks of the Rhine River while on a business trip to Europe, Kimball asked that a perfect replica be created on his mountain in New Hampshire. It took stonemasons two years to complete the project.

The Kimball Castle was passed down from the hands of one Kimball to the next until the 1960s when the last surviving heir of Benjamin Kimball passed away. In her will she left the house, all the property around it, and hundreds of thousands of dollars to a charitable organization with a few stipulations. The grounds must be left intact and turned into a nature preserve and they must never ever turn it into a commercial venture.

The last of Kimball's philanthropical ideals amounted to nothing. The nature preserve was never created, the castle fell into ruin, and a series of legal battles kept the property in stasis for twenty years.

Ultimately, the New Hampshire Attorney General's office took control of the land and offered it to the town of Gilford if they would restore the castle and create the reserve as it was initially intended. Things seemed to be back on track until the tax payers got involved. They felt that a nature preserve sounded like a nice idea; they just didn't want to pay for it, and certainly not take on the expense of restoring a mock Medieval castle to boot. Finally, the attorney general relented and removed the non-commercial development stipulation that the Kimball's had requested. Some of the acreage was subdivided sold and developed. The profit from these sales were used to restore the castle and now the town owns a whopping 260 acres worth of hiking and skiing trails surrounding it.

Hopkinton's Pile of Horseshoes and Other World Records

There are some odd world records out there; the largest cookie, biggest rubber band ball, longest eyebrow, most T-shirts worn at the same time. If you can dream it, likely someone else thought of it before you and made it bigger, taller, smaller, heavier, or more outrageous than you ever thought possible. Thanks to the annual publication of *The Guinness Book of World Records* (a record holder itself, for the best selling copyrighted series of all time), each year more and more people try to top the records of the previous year or try to think up new records to create.

HORSE SHOES ANYONE?

What is probably most interesting about Hopkinton's world record holder, the largest pile of horseshoes in the world, is that it came about accidentally. In 1932, when an old blacksmith's shop was being remodeled, a large amount of old horse shoes were found beneath the floorboards. Instead of discarding the old shoes, they were dumped, haphazardly, into a pile. As years went by, other people in and around Hopkinton began to throw *their* old horse shoes onto the pile and, eventually, it grew to a staggering height. And, of course, once the pile became famous for how big it was, people began to come from all over to see it—and take one or two from the pile as a unique souvenir.

Hopkinton was not in such a hurry to see their horse shoe pile disappear as one might think. As the pile caved in on itself and shrunk, people tried propping it up with various things, wrapped fencing around it, and finally welded together all the bits that weren't rusted together.

Problem solved.

BRIDGES AND GLASSES

New Hampshire is home to several other world records. You'll find the longest covered wooden bridge in the world (it's also the longest double-span wooden bridge in the world) in Cornish.

In 2001, 522 people donned Groucho Marx glasses in Pittsfield, earning the town a world record that it kept for just one year.

But the title that garners the most interest in New Hampshire has to do with Keene and their pumpkins.

KEEN FOR PUMPKINS

Each year, Keene holds a popular pumpkin festival. In 1991, the town hit on a great idea to promote the festivities. It created the Guinness category for "Most pumpkins lit at the same time in one place," and then promptly won themselves the title with an impressive, but not awe inspiring, 1,628 pumpkins. By the time 2003 rolled around, Keene's pumpkin record was newsworthy enough that they earned the title for most pumpkins lit at the same time in one place again, but this time with 28,952 pumpkins. That's five thousand more pumpkins than there are residents in town!

Since then, Keene has started to face some serious competition from, you guessed it, New Hampshire's neighbor to the south, Massachusetts. In 2006, Boston was able to out pumpkin the folks in Keene. Since then, the heat has been on. Each year, Keene and Boston find themselves neck and neck in a race to have the most pumpkins lit as the same time in the same place.

TOSS A PUMPKIN TO WIN!

That isn't the only pumpkin-related world record to be found in New Hampshire. Thanks to Steve, Patrick, Michael and Kathy Seigars, the Granite State town of Greenfield can call itself home to the world record in the trebuchet pumpkin toss category. Never heard of a trebuchet? It's a Medieval war machine, an enormous catapult that was used to heave boulders into the fortresses and castles that were popular forms of defense in the Middle Ages. It involves a carefully weighted swinging wooden arm and was once the scourge of many a Medieval town. The Yankee Siege, as the Seigar crew has dubbed their trebuchet, has secured the pumpkin throwing title every year since 2004. And don't think that is only because no one else has been trying! There are more Medieval-styled war engines out there throwing vegetables than you might think.

The Yankee Siege is designed to throw rocks, up to 250-pound boulders, just like its Dark Ages predecessors, but the Seigars have found pumpkins to be safer and more enjoyable. And just how far can a trebuchet toss an eight to ten pound pumpkin? Well, in 2004, the Yankee Siege won with a 1,394-foot toss. In 2008, they threw a similarly sized gourd 1,897 feet to secure their title.

Each fall, spectators are welcome to trek out to Greenfield and watch them fight to keep their title. It's worth it to make the trip on non-throwing weekends as well. The Yankee Siege is a record winner in its own right, as it is the third largest trebuchet in the world.

DUELING MOUNTAINS

Dueling trebuchets may be an exciting thought, but what about dueling mountains? Japan's Mount Fuji and New Hampshire's Mount Monadnock have been locked in battle for years. What title could Japan's tallest mountain, one of its Three Holy Mountains, possibly be in contention about with the New Hampshire mountain that was written about so favorably by the likes of Ralph Waldo Emerson and Henry David Thoreau?

The worlds most frequently climbed mountain, of course.

A FUNSPOT

Despite the yearly media attention placed on Keene's lit pumpkins, and the mostly good-natured rivalry between it and Boston, those jack o' lanterns really can't hold a candle to what you can find up in Weirs Beach. Located on Lake Winnipesaukee, Weirs Beach is an extremely popular summertime tourist location. And one of the best places for fun for the entire family is at Funspot. Started in 1952, Funspot is much more than a small town arcade.

To begin with, according to the folks at Guinness who are generally considered to be unimpeachable sources for this kind of thing, it is the largest arcade in the world. It even features a Video Game Museum on the third floor. Funspot boasts the largest selection of video games, particularly classic video games, anywhere and this makes it an ideal spot to host the International Classic Video Game and Pinball Tournament. Since the tournament was first to be held here in 1998, Funspot has become the single best place to see professional and/or world championship video game players duke it out via video games. Hundreds, if not thousands, of video game records have been made and broken at Funspot in the past ten years and each year that tally is added to significantly. It is not unusual for a single player to defeat a dozen world records in just one day of tournament play. There are even world records for how many world records a single person has beat in one day at Funspot.

Notorious Graves

New Hampshire may have more than its fair share of haunted cemeteries, but the truly notable graveyards are oftentimes known for much stranger things than a few ghosts.

Riverside Cemetery

Old Tom was steadfast and reliable, a hero of the Civil War who had saved the life of lifelong Alton resident Major George D. Savage on more than one occasion. When he died, the Major requested Tom be buried in Riverside Cemetery in Alton with the full honors and respect he had earned. There was just one problem. Old Tom was a horse.

Several Alton residents didn't care for the idea of a horse getting a full funeral and burial in consecrated ground. George Savage dug in his heels, refusing to back down. In the end, everyone was reasonable about the request. Old Tom did get his funeral at Riverside Cemetery but he was buried just outside the cemetery walls. George Savage could console himself that the horse was on graveyard land and scandalized town residents could console themselves that technically the horse was not buried *in* the cemetery.

Things have changed a lot in all the years that have passed by. Alton has grown and so has its cemetery. The cemetery kept expanding, the walls getting pushed further and further back, and eventually Old Tom's grave was in the middle of the towns cemetery and not just outside it. The horses grave has finally earned its place though. Instead of being an embarrassment, it is well tended and surrounded by a neat white picket fence. The grave itself is marked with a simple rough hewn tombstone that reads:

> Here lies Old Tom
> Charger ridden by
> Maj Geo d. Savage
> on the battlefields
> during the Civil War

If you were wondering, when Major George D. Savage died in February of 1883 he was also buried in Riverside. Savage was buried near Old Tom, though not in the same area designated today by the fence.

CHESTER CEMETERY

Chester Village Cemetery was added to the National Register of Historic Places in 1979 and is thought to be one of the oldest burying grounds in the state. On top of that, it is home to several famous folks. This small cemetery located in the center of Chester, a town of less than 4,000 people, is the final resting spot of two New Hampshire Governors, a New Hampshire Supreme Court Justice, and of Isaac Blaisdell. Isaac Blaisdell may not be a household name today, but he was quite famous as a clock maker in life during the 1700s. Isaac Blaisdell clocks continue to be collectors items that fetch high prices in antique stores.

Historic marker at Chester Village Cemetery.

Chester Village Cemetery is located on Route 102 in Chester, right next door to the town's school and fire department.

Chester's historic Village Cemetery.

But Chester Village Cemetery is more famous for what's on the graves rather than who is in them. Stone carved by a *who's who* of famous stonecutters can be found in the cemetery. Work by John Marble, John Wright, Timothy Eastman, and the Webster brothers are all represented in the small roadside burying ground, making it a haven for gravestone rubbers. However, it's the graves carved by the Webster brothers that get the most attention. Several of the gravestones in this cemetery created by the duo feature faces with less than happy smiles on their faces.

Faces, particularly of angels were common enough graveyard iconography during the Webster's day. Visit any old New England graveyard and you'll see quite a few—each with a beatific grin. But if you want to see some grumpy faces, Chester Village Cemetery is the place to go.

Ask around town and you'll hear a few theories as to why this came about. Some sources say that in his later years Stephen Webster joined an evangelical church and became upset when

he couldn't get his friends and neighbors to convert. Those who rebuffed his spiritual advances in life he cursed with a frown on their tombstones. Other sources say that Stephen Webster was feuding with the town government and the frowns were his way of "voicing" his displeasure.

A quick study of the history of the stones shows instantly that Stephen Webster carved the frowns. His brother Abel's creations all have the expected grins. But why this is, is most likely to remain a mystery.

Old Burying Ground

This cemetery in Jaffrey is the final resting place of Willa Cather. Cather was born in Nebraska and made her name writing stories of frontier life on the Great Plains; one of these works, *One of Ours*, would win Cather the Pulitzer Prize in 1923. Later she became a resident of Pittsburgh and New York City. So why is she buried in a small New England cemetery?

Willa Cather visited Jaffrey for the first time in 1917. Almost immediately she declared it as a place where she could write. After this first trip, Cather would make Jaffrey an annual stop in her travels. Most of her Pulitzer Prize winning novel and *My Antonia*, widely held to be the most popular of her works, were written in a tent erected in a large field in Jaffrey that had a fine view of Mount Monadnock.

Shortly before her death, Cather asked that her body be shipped to Jaffrey for burial. She even specified the cemetery she wanted to be buried in and where. Her gravestone sits at the edge of the cemetery, in a wooded area near several rhododendron bushes.

PINE HILL CEMETERY

Pine Hill Cemetery is better known as the haunted Blood Cemetery (and stories about its hauntings can be found elsewhere in this book). But Pine Hill Cemetery, in Hollis, is a real treat for people who aren't trying to find ghosts, too. The reason for this is that many of the older graves feature interesting little poetic verses instead of the usual "Beloved Mother," "Beloved Son" type of epitaphs on their gravestone.

One such grave, marking the final resting spot of Rebecca Alexanders (died 1799) reads:

> Behold my friends as you pass by
> As you are now so once was I
> As I am now you soon must be
> Prepare for death and follow me

A similarly jaunty rhyme can be found on the 1810 tombstone of Caleb Farley:

> Friends and Physicians could not save
> My mortal body from the grave

Nor can the grave confine me here
When Christ shall call me to appear

The inscripted gravestones are the ones most often targeted by vandals, which are an even greater plague at this cemetery than most. Oftentimes, when these older graves are heavily vandalized, they are not repairable and are, instead, replaced with much simpler tombstones. So many of the poetic graves have already been lost and more and more disappear each year.

OLD NORTH CEMETERY

Franklin Pierce is the only United States President, to date, to hail from New Hampshire. In life Pierce was known for being easy going, which won him many allies in Washington, and an electoral landslide. Pierce, a true dark-horse candidate if there ever was one, got 254 votes in the electoral college, compared to only 42 for the Whig party candidate Winfield Scott.

But Pierce's popularity didn't last. Most often, personal troubles are credited with destroying his ability to be an effective President. Just two months before his inauguration, he witnessed the train accident that killed his son, aged only eleven at the time. Pierce's other two children were already deceased at this point. Franklin Pierce's wife, Jane, seemed to have suffered from debilitating depression, no doubt linked to the deaths of all three of her children. She came from a long line of Whig party members, who were horrified to have her married to a Democrat even if he was President. She hated politics, and despised living in Washington, D.C. Jane wanted nothing more than for her husband to resign and to return to his New Hampshire law practice.

These family issues, coupled with a series of unpopular political decisions, seemed to have all but paralyze Pierce. He sought, but did not win, his party's nomination the next election year. Despite how highly regarded he was thought of as a lawyer and as a state politician, Pierce has gone down in history as one of the nation's least popular and one of the most incompetent Presidents.

Franklin Pierce died in Concord on October 8, 1869. He is buried in Concord's Old North Burying Ground in a family plot.

OLD BURYING GROUND

This is the second cemetery in the list of notable New Hampshire graveyards to bear the name "Old Burying Grounds" but you don't have to worry that anyone will confuse the two. One is located in Jaffrey. This one can be found on Faxen Hill Road in Washington. One is famous for being the burial spot of famed American author Willa Cather. This Old Burying Ground is most famous for being the burial spot of one leg.

In 1804, Captain Samuel Jones lost his leg in an accident and had the appendage buried in a plot in Old Burying Ground. He even had a tombstone erected for the amputated limb, Engraved on the simple stone monument are the straightforward enough words: "Captain Samuel Jones leg which was amputated July 7, 1804."

Stranger still, the rest of Samuel Jones' body cannot be found at Old Burying Ground. When he died, he was buried in Boston, with no mention of the lost leg.

Looking up from the gravestone of Samuel Jones' leg, the first thing you see is a large marble ball. This too is a grave marker. And who lies under this uncommon tombstone? The name underneath says only the name "BALL."

But you shouldn't think that the Ball family is the only funny grave there is to be found in this cemetery in Washington. The title of funniest and most ironic gravestone would have to go to the final resting place of Fred and Elba Chase. In the 1930s, the Chases would be very active members of the Communist party. In an effort to hasten the arrival of Communism into their little part of the world, the Chases would run for political offices. Elba, apparently a feminist as well as a communist, ran for New Hampshire Governor in 1938. One can't help but think that she was not surprised when she lost. Her husband had run for the place of United States Senator from New Hampshire six years earlier and had also been defeated.

The Chases tombstone declares them as:

"Courageous and Devoted Fighters in the Class Struggle"

It is also engraved with a Soviet hammer and sickle.

What's so ironic about that? The Chase tombstone is by far the largest in the cemetery, overshadowing all the stone around them. The Chases, or someone in their family, must have spent a great deal of money to make sure they were so prominently remembered after a life of championing the cause of an egalitarian society.

Graves with engraved fingers pointing up were very popular for a period of time.

METHODIST CEMETERY

In the 1860s and 1870s it was a common piece of graveyard iconography to have a finger engraved on ones tombstone pointing up, which was hopefully the direction you'd find your soul traveling in when the time came.

Ira Bowles, whose grave can be found in Whitefield's Methodist Cemetery, passed on in 1863—a prime time to end up with a pointing finger as your last message to the world. And Ira Bowles does have a finger on his grave. The only problem is that Ira's finger is pointing *down*.

He's not the only Whitefield resident to get such a strange moniker. Henry Lane, whose grave can be found in the Pine Street Cemetery also has a downward pointing finger.

It is unclear why these two men have the finger pointing the wrong way, whether they earned it or it was an accident. But considering one died in 1863 and the other in 1866, it seems likely that the same man must be responsible for both graves, whatever his reasoning may have been.

PEOPLE

CHIEF PASSACONAWAY

The earliest inhabitants of most of New Hampshire were the Penacook Indians. The Penacooks were a part of the Algonquin tribe and could be found throughout northern Massachusetts on up to southern Maine, along with the large swatch of south eastern New Hampshire found in between. At their height, the tribe consisted of somewhere around 12,000 individuals, though they were split up into two dozen different villages, and the Penacooks were semi-nomadic.

The spot where the city of Manchester stands today was once an important place to many of these bands of Penacooks. Amoskeag Falls, the reason why Manchester would later become an important textile manufacturing center in the world, was just as important to the success and lifestyle of the Penacooks. There was an enormous number of fish just around the falls, enough so that the tribe not only existed mainly on a high protein fish diet, but they were able to use their catch to fertilize their two biggest crops, corn and tobacco.

At the time, when the first white explorers began to trickle into New Hampshire, the Penacooks were led by the great chief Passaconaway. In the native tongue his name meant "Child of the bear" and the name was a fitting one for him. Passaconaway made his name, firstly, as a great hero in the wars that the Penacooks fought against the neighboring Micmac tribe. Later, Passaconaway would become known as much for his wisdom as for his prowess in battle.

There was always something supernatural surrounding this great chief. There were as many legends told about the chief while he was still alive as are normally made up about great figures after they die. The stories the natives told about him that survive to this day tell of his ability to restore green life to long dead plants; they also said that he could handle snakes without being bitten, and even that he caused water to freeze or to unfreeze with just a touch of his hand.

"Like the budding of spring leaves, they come in great numbers." Passaconaway warned his people when the first white settlements began to appear in southern New Hampshire.

Passaconaway was, perhaps, among the first of the Native American chiefs to realize that life as his people had known it for countless generations could not continue on in the face of this influx of new people. As hunting grew tougher and the old ways of the Native's began to give way under pressure from these new neighbors, other tribes felt they just had to tough things out for awhile and that the settlers could somehow be implored to leave. Passaconaway knew better. He knew that the Natives would have to change their ways or perish, assimilate at least a little or die out completely. Although there is little actual proof of this, and we do know that Passaconaway did not convert himself, legend says that it was Passaconaway who invited a missionary named John Elliott to come to Amoskeag Falls and preach the Christian religion to his tribe.

As the town of Manchester, called Derryfield at this point, began to grow along the Merrimack River, the fishing grew worse for the Penacooks who so depended on it. It became harder and harder for the them to gather enough food to feed their whole tribe. Passaconaway was growing old, and he knew that his time as leader was over. He called together the people of his tribe and gave a rousing speech, pleading with them to make peace with the white settlers and adapt to the new world that was dawning around them. Passaconaway then handed the leadership of the tribe over to his son.

"Peace," he implored his people. "Peace is the only hope of our race."

Lake Massabesic, as seen from Auburn, was an important fishing location for the Native American tribes that preceded the white settlers in this region.

Soon after this speech, Passaconaway took his canoe down to Lake Massabesic and started to paddle towards Loon Island. It was a place that was said to hold memories of happier times for the aging chief, and is one of several islands that dot the surface of the lake to this day.

The day was bright and warm, but as Chief Passaconaway rowed towards the small island, the sky grew black and the lake started to roil. The whole thing was so unusual that the tribe started to gather along the shore to see if they could figure out what was going on. Lightning flashed endlessly, blinding the crowd, and the first small drops of rain began to strike the surface of the lake. Somehow, everyone gathered could sense that their holy spirit, Kichtou Manitou, was the one causing the upheaval. Passaconaway threw down his paddle and stood up in the flailing boat, raising his hands towards the darkening sky. Legend says that suddenly there was a flash of light, far brighter then that of ordinary lightning. In an instant the dark cloud had passed, the sun peaked out its rays again. As quickly as it had darkened the day, once more it became bright. But when the tribe looked for Passaconaway, both he and his canoe were gone. Somehow in the brief instant of light they had vaporized into nothingness.

Today, Lake Massabesic supplies water for nearly 125,000 Manchester area residents. It has even become a popular tourist spot. Because it's used for drinking water, swimming is prohibited

Lake Massabesic, a popular fishing and ghost hunting spot.

and boating is carefully regulated. The New Hampshire Department of Fish and Game keep the lake well stocked with trout and it is one of the best places in the northeast to catch small mouth bass and yellow perch. But some visitors to the area catch more then a ten-pound bass while at Lake Massabesic; some catch a glimpse of the great Chief Passaconaway as well.

The ghost of Chief Passaconaway manifests itself in several ways. In the more then 200 years since he died, many people have reported seeing an incredible man, his face heavily wrinkled and careworn, but with a peaceful smile, wrapped in a homespun blanket in a rough-hewn canoe on the waters of Lake Massabesic. They say that if you take your eyes off of him for even the briefest of moments, that when you look again, he has disappeared without a trace, much as Passaconaway was said to have disappeared on the day he lost his life.

Oftentimes, when looking out towards Loon Island you can see a rainbow, in the shape of a circle, in the sky above the island.

Legend says that this is a sign of the Native American warrior watching over the lands his tribe once owned. The spirit doesn't seem to bother the fish any though, several fisherman have said that the best fishing in the area is right off the shores of Loon Island, in the spots where Great Chief Passaconaway is seen most often.

THE EXECUTION OF RUTH BLAY

South Cemetery is the general term used for a collection of five closely placed graveyards in Portsmouth. The five cemeteries that make up South Cemetery are Auburn Cemetery, Cotton's Cemetery, Harmony Grove Cemetery, Proprietors' Burying Ground

South Cemetery is at the same location as one of the last executions in the state of New Hampshire.

and Sagamore Cemetery. The first of these five graveyards was begun as far back as 1671 and many of the old tombstones can still be seen today, fighting for their place among the modern-day gravestones. South Cemetery is known as a haunted place but it also has important ties to New Hampshire history . . . and this is the sort of past you won't normally find mentioned in the history books.

In 1768, the hottest scandal of the day concerned a young unmarried school teacher by the name of Ruth Blay. It was discovered that the twenty-five year old Blay had given birth to an illegitimate child, one she swore was still born, and had then buried the infants body beneath the floorboards of her Portsmouth school room. Whether the child was actually still born, died from Blay delivering the child herself, or was outright murdered by the frightened young lady didn't matter in the least. At this time, there were a good 600 crimes in New Hampshire that could result in the death penalty. Concealing the birth and death of an illegitimate child was a crime in and of itself and it was certainly taken seriously. Two other Portsmouth women, Sarah Simpson and Penelope Kenny, had been executed for the same crime less than thirty years before the Blay incident. The court case against Blay was decided quickly and, like Kenny and Simpson before her, Ruth Blay was sentenced to hang.

Surprisingly, on the day of the execution thousands of people poured into Portsmouth to show their support for the school teacher. The death sentence was wildly unpopular and public sentiment was firmly on the side of Ruth. As the cart carried the prisoner to the gallows the crowd began to chant for her to be let go.

According to legend and to some old newspaper accounts, as the clock ticked down to hanging time, the Governor did issue a reprieve to the young school teacher. But in a final twist of fate it did not reach her in time. Despite hearing that the Governor was reconsidering the matter, Sheriff Thomas Packer, who wanted to get things over with so as to not delay his supper, hung Ruth Blay as

You won't find a tombstone for Ruth Blay in South Cemetery. Her grave lies unmarked and unknown.

quickly as possible. Another crowd would later form to hang Sheriff Packer in effigy, but of course by that point it made no difference to the dead.

After Ruth Blay was hung, her body was removed from the gallows and buried in an unmarked grave. Today South Cemetery covers the spot of her execution and, some say, her unmarked grave.

Perhaps because of the way she was wronged in life or because of the further insult of being buried in an unmarked grave, the ghost of Ruth Blay is supposed to roam South Cemetery. She is most often felt in the area around the South Street entrance to the burying grounds. Visitors report feeling as though something cold was plucking at their clothing, almost as if trying to lead them somewhere, or to keep them from going away from a certain spot.

EUNICE "GOODY" COLE

There was a lot that could be said about Goody Cole. She was a firm believer in antinomianism, which is the idea that Christians are under no religious, civic, or moral obligation to follow the laws of any Government or even any religious authorities. She had a fierce temper that was the scourge of her neighbors. Joseph Dow, author of *History of the Town of Hampton, NH*, has said of Eunice Cole " . . . she was both hated and feared" and "She was said to be, ill-natured and ugly, artful and aggravating, malicious and revengeful." It was said she would go out of her way to be disagreeable to just about anyone, followed no social niceties, and not even the most basic of what was considered "good manners." Keeping these things in mind, it is probably not surprising that she is famous even today, over 500 years after her life and death, as being the Witch of Hampton.

Her religious views were so unpopular, and she was particularly outspoken about them, that she was brought to court many times for giving what they called at the time slanderous speeches, and that today we would probably just consider it as free speech. From 1645 to 1656, town records show at least a dozen court cases she had to attend to defend herself, and at times, she was brought as far south as Boston to take responsibility for something or other she said. She was convicted from time to time, but Eunice Cole never learned her lesson. She went in shouting about her beliefs and came out the same way.

In 1656, a new kind of accusation was thrown Cole's way, one of witchcraft. It is hard to say today if anyone really believed that she was a witch at the time or if they felt they had just finally struck on a charge that would silence her for good. The evidence against Goody Cole was about as damning as any of the evidence given against anyone accused of witch craft during that time period. That is to say it was completely circumstantial and yet still impossible to defend ones self against. Some of the most damning evidence depended solely on the law of averages. Given her legendary dislike for people, it was perhaps ironic that Goody Cole had a well on her property that was a popular stop for travelers. She was known to stand at her stoop and holler insults at the people who partook of the waters from her well. And some of these people, further down the road, months or even years later, would face hardships and bad luck. During her trial, one person after another lined up to testify that Cole's curses at the well were real curses and that she must be in league with the devil to wield such power.

Later on at the trial, a neighbor stood up and said that once his cows had wandered onto Cole's property. Incensed she had

Hampton's Tuck Museum now stands nearby the place where Goody Cole spent her last years. It is also home to one of her memorials.

yelled at him to get his cows off her lawn or they'd choke on each blade of grass they stole from her. He removed the cows as quickly as possible, but later on one of the calves died and months later one disappeared. Clearly, this neighbor felt at least, that Cole's curse had come true. Some of the strongest evidence against Cole was given by a group of school children, who told wild tales about devil dwarves of some type.

Needless to say Cole was convicted. But the courts were, for the time period, quite lenient on her. Technically, she could have been executed for her crimes. Instead, she was sentenced to a whipping and life in jail. In fact, Goody Cole dodged the witchcraft bullet more than once. She ended up being released and then convicted several more times before her death. She was to be the only

This unmarked stone located outside of the Tuck Museum is a memorial to the now exonerated Goody Cole.

woman convicted of witchcraft in New Hampshire's history. Each time Goody Cole left prison, she returned to Hampton, living in poorer conditions each time, until finally she ended up shunned and alone in a shack at the bottom of Rand's Hill near where Hampton's Tuck Museum can be found today.

When she died, the story goes, her body was dragged from the filthy shack where she spent her golden years and buried in a nearby ditch. Before interring the body, her neighbors drove a stake through her heart and hung an iron horseshoe atop it to keep the devil away. The grave was left unmarked, far from any cemeteries, and to this day has not been found. There are two "gravestone" memorials to Goody Cole in Hampton, but neither marks where her body is actually buried.

Goody Cole was gone, but not forgotten. In 1939, with Eunice Cole dead in an unmarked grave for hundreds of years long passed, the residents of Hampton voted in favor of exonerating her of her charges. The official court documents condemning her as witch were burned on Hampton Beach and, mixed with soil from the area where her home stood, they were placed in an urn that can still be seen today at the Tuck Museum.

It says something about the power of a bad reputation that Goody Cole's memorials are unmarked and unadvertised today. Ghosts stories abound about the lady, and the markers became a target for vandals. Many people say they have been approached by a wild-haired woman, in ragged old-fashioned clothing, in the oldest parts of town. Some have even spoken with the woman who they say asks continually about the whereabouts of some of Hampton's oldest families. In the 1950s, a housewife saw this apparition, never realizing it was a ghost, and invited the woman inside for some lemonade. The little old woman started yelling about not being able to find the Goody Cole memorial on the village green and the housewife told her that it hadn't been erected yet. At this point, the old woman thanked her for the lemonade and walked out of the house—straight through the closed front door!

The witch's ghost can still be seen in and around Founder's Park. Some people say they have felt her long bony fingers pinching them and slapping at them when they walked across the grass. This has led to some speculation that her body may have been buried in the vicinity of the park. She has also been seen, and felt, in the main building of the Tuck Museum outside of which her memorial can be found.

COMMODORE NUTT

Phineas Taylor Barnum, better known of course as P.T. Barnum, is about as famous for his fabulous hoaxes and scams as he is for founding the circus that would come to bear the name Ringling Brothers and Barnum & Bailey Circus. A businessman, a showman, and consummate entertainer, Barnum is known for having said, "Never attempt to catch a whale with a minnow." This is a somewhat ironic statement considering Barnum made a whale of a fortune, off of leviathan-sized crowds that flocked in to see some very small people. A large part of Barnum's fabulous fortune was made promoting and showing two men, neither of whom would grow to top four feet in height. One of these men was Charles Sherwood Stratton, who was billed under the stage name of "General Tom Thumb;" the other was Manchester, New Hampshire, born George Washington Morrison Nutt, aka Commodore Nutt.

Nutt was born in Manchester on April 1, 1844, to normal-sized parents; in fact, his father, Rodnia, was said to be a rather large man, well over six feet tall and nearly three hundred pounds. But it soon become apparent that George was not going to following in his fathers very large footsteps. The type of dwarfism that caused Nutt's short stature was most likely genetic, as most cases of dwarfism are. But the condition was said to be unknown in the families of Nutt's parents and they were, undoubtedly, surprised to have such a small son after having several average-sized children.

George's small size became only more and more noticeable as he got older and it garnered him a lot of attention in the city of Manchester. In time, word about the youth spread far enough that the family was approached by a manager by the name of Lillie. Lillie soon had the boy touring from one side of New England to the other, oftentimes charging crowds the paltry sum of five cents to see him. Even as mismanaged as the boy seemed to be under Lillie, George was getting enough media attention that, by the 1860s, P.T. Barnum became aware of the boy and dedicated himself to taking over his stage career. By this time, Barnum had already achieved much success showing the dwarf known as General Tom Thumb. Barnum thought little of Lillie's management prowess. He felt the boy's education was lacking, that he could be earning more money, and that all in all Lillie didn't "understand doing this thing up in the *proper style*."

After much finagling Barnum did become Nutt's manager. It could even be said that Barnum got two Nutt's for the price of one, as Rodnia refused to let the boy go on a nationwide tour unless accompanied by his older brother, Rodnia, Jr. Barnum started off calling the boy the "$30,000 Nut," thirty thousand supposedly being the amount he paid to the Nutt family for the boy. In truth, the child was paid $12 a week, with free room and board, and a small percentage of profits from any souvenir items. The wage gap between what he said he paid and what he was actually paying did not bother Barnum at all. He felt it was fine to deceive the public so long as they got something of value for their interest and money. At the time Nutt signed on with Barnum he was close to twenty-nine inches tall and not quite twenty-five pounds in weight.

Often advertised as "the smallest man in the world," Nutt flourished under Barnum's tutelage. Much like Tom Thumb before him Nutt would go on to achieve much fame and fortune under Barnum. Already planning to show Nutt with "General" Tom Thumb, Barnum dubbed the youth "Commodore."

Despite his world travels, Commodore Nutt requested his body be returned to Merrill Cemetery in Manchester for burial.

Nutt family graves in Merrill Cemetery.

Shortly after debuting in Barnum's famous museum in New York, Commodore Nutt was invited to the White House to meet President Lincoln. Even though they arrived in the middle of a cabinet meeting, Nutt was brought before Lincoln without delay. Quipping on his guest's small size, Lincoln is said to have advised the "Commodore" that if he were ever to find himself in danger while commanding his ships, he should wade ashore. Nutt is said to have looked pointedly at the President's long legs and replied, "I guess, Mr. President, you could do that better than I."

President Lincoln would not be the only notable figure Commodore Nutt would meet thanks to Barnum. He soon found himself on a world-wide tour along with Tom Thumb. On this tour, Nutt would go, by invitation, before royalty in countries across the globe. He, and the other dwarfs in Barnum's retinue, were known throughout the world, ate at the finest restaurants, and achieved the status of celebrities.

Eventually, Commodore Nutt would split from Barnum and take over his own career. In the 1870s, Nutt would marry. George Nutt would die from Brights disease, a historic catch-all term referring to several types of kidney disease, in 1881. George Nutt died in New York City. His body was brought back to New Hampshire for burial in Merrill Cemetery on South Willow Street in Manchester.

Old photos of Madame Sherri, along with her biography, mark the entrance to the hiking trails located on what was once her home.

MADAME ANTOINETTE SHERRI

The woman who would ultimately become legend in New Hampshire history as 'Madame Sherri," began life as Antoinette De Lilas. In the early 1900s, she was a cabaret singer in Paris, growing accustomed to haute couture, fine foods and drink, and everything else the French nightlife had to offer a beautiful vivacious young woman. For reasons unknown, in 1911, Antoinette left Paris and headed out to New York City. She was at this point married to Andre Riele. Riele, a silent film star, would convince Antoinette to change their names to Sherri when they reached the shore of the United States.

In New York, the newly christened Sherri would start a very successful costume business that designed clothes for theatre shows such as the Ziegfeld Follies. Antoinette, always on top of the fashions and with an eye for beauty, was the creative force behind the venture. Things seemed to be going well for the couple.

But nothing lasts forever and tragedy soon struck. Antoinette's husband, significantly younger than she, died unexpectedly in 1924. Shocked by the death of her husband, Antoinette decided to give up on New York. She had, by this point, amassed a fortune. The wealthy young widow could have traveled anywhere in the world. Paris, London, Madrid, any of the world's major cities would have welcomed her with open arms. Instead, she decided to move to New Hampshire. With her husband she had spent several vacations in the Granite State and Spofford Lake was at the time a popular retreat for theatre folk.

Sherri soon found a large plot of farmland in Chesterfield and had a fanciful fifteen-room mansion built that she liked to call her castle. But Sherri did not settle down to a life of a widowed farmer. Her castle became a hot spot and her summer bashes became legendary. She was an iconic figure around town. And much talked about. Sherri did nothing to try and deflect the attention she attracted. She could be seen nearly daily being driven apparently aimlessly around the small town in her chauffeur driven Packard. She was known for traveling around the area wearing a fur coat— and nothing else—in even the worst summer heat. Topping things off, literally, Sherri was accompanied on these aimless trips by her pet monkey. This exotic pet sat primly on Sherris' shoulder (atop the fur coat, in the chauffeur-driven Packard) while she stroked its fur and fed it small bites of food carefully prepared by her private cook.

This overgrown gatepost is what remains of the carefully landscaped entrance to Sherri's Castle.

It is not surprising that her castle was soon dubbed a brothel by scandalized local town folk and that she was soon referred to as Madame Sherri rather than Antoinette. But the scorn and gossip of her neighbors was soon the least of Sherri's worries. Her fortune dwindled and she eventually ended up destitute, alone, and confined to a state-run nursing home in Brattleboro, Vermont. Her once luxurious castle fell into disrepair and became a popular place for vandals, drawn by the ruined splendor and the now legendary gossip about the place. The building would be almost entirely gutted by a fire set by unidentified arsons in 1962.

Path leading to the ruins of Sherri's Castle.

All that survives from the fire and the ravages of time are parts of the stone foundation, a fireplace, and part of a grand staircase that local high school kids have renamed the "Stairway to Heaven." Each year sees these stone structures lose their shape a little more and it becomes harder and harder to even imagine the enormous home that once flourished around them.

The haunted staircase.

Vandals and the curious are still often found at the remains of Madame Sherri's castle. Today they are less drawn by the stories of wild orgies than they are by the ghost stories. Touching what remains of the staircase is said to start up the faint sound of long ago waltzing music. Even the spirit of Sherri herself is said to make an appearance from time to time. The transparent, though clearly visible, shape of a glamorous woman has been seen—both with and without her fur coat! Many visitors to the former castle say she has approached them, the eternal hostess, as though welcoming to her home for a party.

What remains of the grand fireplace.

Today, hikers enjoy Madam Sherri's forest instead of theater folk and artists.

FUNNY NEW HAMPSHIRE
PART ONE

New Hampshire is known for many things. The rousing "Live Free or Die" state motto, for instance. Or for the states lack of sales or income taxes. Or driving a motorcycle without a helmet. Or large state-run liquor stores conveniently located just over the state border shared with Massachusetts (as pointed out in the *Simpsons* episode where a "Welcome to New Hampshire" sign has a smaller sign beneath it reading "Providing Cheap Liquor to Massachusetts Teens for 200 Years." D'oh!) But, despite the *Simpsons'* nod, "hilarious" isn't one of the common stereotypes people think of when they think of New Hampshire.

Maybe we need to adjust our stereotypes. New Hampshire abounds with funny people. Bob Montana, creator of the *Archie* comic strip, attended Manchester High School and lived most of his adult life in Meredith, New Hampshire, where his daughters live to this day.

New Hampshire can also lay claim to several *Saturday Night Live* alumni. Seth Myers, one of the shows head writers and anchor of its weekly "Weekend Update" news skit, was born and raised in Bedford. Also from Bedford is Sarah Silverman, who wrote for *Saturday Night Live* for just one season before going on to host her own show on Comedy Central. But probably the most famous of New Hampshire's *Saturday Night Live* comedians is Adam Sandler. The funny man moved to Manchester at the age of five and spent his childhood there. And Sandler certainly hasn't forgotten his Granite State roots. He is known for his charitable donations to Manchester institutions.

The oddest comedian link New Hampshire can lay claim to is as the watery resting place of George Carlin. Carlin was a comedian known for tackling taboo subjects, such as religion or politics, most often using the most colorful language possible. He is, perhaps, most famous for a comedy routine known as "Carlin's Seven Dirty Words," a monologue about the words that are considered to be so vile you will never hear them on television. Carlin should have added "or radio" onto that title because a radio broadcast of the routine would lead to a Supreme Court Case that helped decide just how much control the Government had over our rights to free speech. Carlin was the first host of *Saturday Night Live*, a frequent guest on just about any late night talk show you can think of, and would have his own sitcom for awhile.

Carlin was born in New York City but he did not want to be returned there to be buried when he died. In fact, Carlin didn't want to be buried at all. His final wishes were to be cremated and for his ashes to be scattered outside several of the comedy clubs that had been so important to him when he was starting off his career in the comedy business. The one exception to this was a request from the late great funny man that some of those ashes be put aside to be scattered at Spofford Lake.

Why Spofford Lake? As a child, Carlin had spent several summers at a now defunct camp located along the shores of the 739-acre Spofford Lake. The lake, apparently, was as important to the life of the comedian as a young man as the comedy clubs were later on in life.

HUMPHREY BOGART

The Portsmouth Naval Prison is an imposing building that can be easily seen from just about anywhere on Portsmouth's waterfront. It is located within the Piscataqua River directly between the cities of Portsmouth and Kittery, and in 2001, it was the subject of a border dispute between the states of Maine and New Hampshire. The Prison is an imposing grandiose structure,

His fond memories of childhood summers prompted comedian George Carlin to request that his ashes be scattered here at Spofford Lake.

built in the early part of the 1900s and added onto several times over the years it was in operation, this 265,000 square foot prison is more commonly known as "The Castle" or the "Alcatraz of the East" due to its distinctive appearance and because no inmate ever successfully was able to escape. The inability to escape the Prison had more to do with rumors than towering walls. There was a persistent myth during the time it was used as a prison that any guard who had a prisoner escape on his watch would be doomed to finish out the criminals sentence. It was not, by any means, true but the story was believed enough that the guards were extra diligent while performing their duties.

While serving in the Navy, Bogart was ordered to bring a prisoner to Portsmouth by train from Boston. Just as they reached Portsmouth the handcuffed prisoner asked Bogart for a cigarette. As Bogart went to light the cigarette dangling from the prisoners lip the man saw his chance. He bashed Bogart in the face with his handcuffs and started running. Bogart's lip was badly ripped and, plastic surgery being what is was at the time, there was not much that could be done to restore his lip. Thus Bogart ended up with his distinctive lip sneer.

MARILLA RICKER

In the November 2008 elections, New Hampshire found it suddenly had a female majority Senate. In fact, the thirteen ladies of the New Hampshire Senate make up the first female majority legislative body in the entire country. But the achievements of these women in the male-dominated world of politics has a history in the state that reaches much further back than many suspect.

Marilla M. Ricker always considered herself lucky to have been raised by a father who didn't discriminate when it came to his daughter. She had the same kind of education and opportunities he would have given to any son. And Ricker made sure she put that education and freedom to good use.

After finding herself widowed after only five years of marriage, Ricker had legal privileges she would not have had as a married women. She was, for instance, allowed to own her own property and be responsible for her own financial affairs. This was important considering that her father and husband had left her substantial inheritances that ensured she would never have to be under anyone's thumb.

Marilla Ricker used some of this money to attend the first ever National Women's Suffrage Convention in Washington, D.C. There she heard the greatest women of her age speak out against the country's unfair patriarchical system. The speakers at the convention implored the women in attendance to start locally rather than wait for a national change.

Ricker seems to have taken what she heard at the convention to heart. She returned home, appeared at the Dover town hall, and asked for her name to be added to the voting checklist. But, three days later when she appeared at the same town hall to vote, she found her name was stricken from the list. Women, of course, we not allowed to vote. Shrewdly, Ricker inquired how the town could tax her.

"If taxation without representation was tyranny before the Revolutionary War, it is tyranny today," she argued.

The Dover selectmen were unmoved. Ricker was not allowed to vote and she paid her taxes under protest. But she was not swayed either. Ricker came back the next year with the same argument and the year after that. Finally, trying to placate the woman, Dover allowed her to vote. The problem was that while her vote was accepted by the town it was not counted towards the results. But Ricker would not be so easily quieted.

While maintaining her home in Dover as a summer place she moved to Washington, D.C. There she would study law and, in 1882, become the first women from New Hampshire to be admitted to the bar. She took the test with eighteen other people, all men, and passed with the highest grade of any of them.

As a lawyer, Ricker was known for championing the rights of prisoners and the poor. She would even hire and pay for another lawyer for her clients if time restraints kept her from personally taking their case. And Ricker certainly was busy. She was active in politics, applied to be the first female U.S. Ambassador (though McKinley passed her by for the job), and was an outspoken figure in the women's rights movement. Her direct way of talk never failed. She was famous for trying to make the case that women could not be convicted of crimes since all the statutes used the word "he" and because women could not vote.

"So long as women are hanged under the laws, they should have a voice in making them," Ricker was known to say. It was an unpopular opinion for the time.

In 1889, she successfully petitioned the New Hampshire Supreme Court to open the practice of law in the state to women. Less successful was her campaign to become Governor of New Hampshire. Though she applied and paid the necessary fees to do so, the courts, due to her gender, resoundingly rejected her right to have her name on the ballot.

Ricker died in Dover. Her work paved the way for the women of her time as well as though who came after her. In 1997, the New Hampshire House and Senate passed a motion to have Marilla M. Ricker's portrait hung prominently in the Statehouse as acknowledgment of her work in the state and beyond.Design: box or side bar the jokes (or make them stand out in some way)

APPENDIX

NEW HAMPSHIRE FAST FACTS

State capital: Concord

Became a state: New Hampshire was the ninth state to join the Union, doing so on June 21, 1788

State motto: Live free or die

State nickname: The Granite State

State flower: purple lilac

State bird: purple finch

State tree: paper birch or white birch

State dog: the Chinook, the only dog breed known to have originated in the state and the rarest breed of dog in the world according to such sources such as the *Guinness Book of World Records* and the American Kennel Club.

Highest point in New Hampshire: Mt. Washington at 6,288 feet

FAMOUS NEW HAMPSHIRE

NEW HAMPSHIRE ON THE BIG SCREEN

MOVIES FILMED IN THE GRANITE STATE:

Affliction (Concord and Pembroke)
A Separate Peace (Exeter)
The Cider House Rules (Hampton Falls)
The Good Son (North Conway)
In Dreams (New Castle)
Jumanji (Keene and Swanzey)
Little Women (Concord)
On Golden Pond (Holderness)
The Shining (Bretton Woods)
The Skulls (Hanover)
The Thomas Crown Affair (Salem)

FAMOUS GRANITE STATERS

A brief look at some of the people who have claimed New Hampshire home at some point in their notable lives:

Amy Beach (musician)
Ralph Baer (Inventor of the concept of video games)
Dan Brown (writer)
Ken Burns (Documentary filmmaker)
Chris Carpenter (baseball player)

Salmon P. Chase (Secretary of the U.S. treasury and chief justice of the U.S. Supreme Court)

Barbara Ann Cochran (Olympic gold medalist in slalom skiing)

E.E. Cummings (poet)

Mary Baker Eddy (founder of the Christian Science religion and The Christian Science Monitor)

William Pitt Fessenden (U.S. Senator)

Carlton Fisk (baseball player)

Mike Flanagan (baseball player)

Elizabeth Gurley Flynn (helped found the American Civil Liberties Union)

Sam Walter Foss (writer)

Robert Frost (poet)

Rene Gagnon (U.S. Marine seen in Raising the Flag on Iwo Jima)

Horace Greeley (founder and publisher of the *New York Tribune*)

Sarah Josepha Hale (magazine editor and writer)

Donald Hall (poet)

John Irving (writer)

Dean Kamen (inventor)

Maxine Kumin (writer)

Dudley Leavitt (publisher)

Paul Michael Levesque (aka Triple H, wrestler)

Christa McAuliffe (teacher, strength)

Richard and Maurice McDonald (creators of the original McDonalds restaurant)

Grace Metalious (writer)

Seth Meyers (comedian)

Bode Miller (professional skier)

Bob Montana (creator of *Archie* comic strip)

Mandy Moore (singer, actress)

P.J. O'Rourke (writer)

Maxfield Parrish (artist)
Jodi Picoult (writer)
Franklin Pierce (14th President of the United States)
Eleanor Porter (writer)
Charles Revson (founder of Revlon cosmetics)
Red Rolfe (baseball player)
J.D. Salinger (writer)
Adam Sandler (comedian)
Alan Shepard Jr. (astronaut)
Sarah Silverman (comedian)
David Souter (associate justice of the United States Supreme Court)
Jennifer Thompson (Olympic champion)
Earl Tupper (creator of Tupperware)

FUNNY NEW HAMPSHIRE PART TWO

New Englanders in general are thought to have a kind of odd sense of humor and, as part of the New England states, New Hampshire is no different. A word of warning though—many of our jokes poke (gentle) fun at our neighbors.

Four men are driving in a car together. There is one from Maine, one from Vermont, one from Massachusetts, and one from New Hampshire. All of a sudden the man from Maine rolls down his window and starts throwing bags of potatoes out of the car saying, "We have so many potatoes; I'm just sick and tired of seeing these things."

A little further up the road the man from Vermont starts throwing jugs of maple syrup out of the car window saying, "We have so much maple syrup in Vermont we've just got to get rid of some of it."

Inspired, the man from New Hampshire opens up the door and rolls the man from Massachusetts out of the car . . . .

Some surveyors working along the New Hampshire and Maine border realize that the state lines are off and decide to move the boundaries a little. On their way home they stop to tell a farmer that he is no longer in Maine but now resides in New Hampshire.

"Good," says the farmer. "I couldn't take another one of those Maine winters."

And finally, you know you're in New Hampshire when . . .

You often switch from "heat" to "A/C" in the same day and back again. You use a down comforter in the summer.

You drive at 65 mph through 2 feet of snow during a raging blizzard, without flinching.

You install security lights on your house and garage and leave both unlocked.

You define summer as three months of bad sledding.

You can recognize someone from Massachusetts from their driving.

You know where Contoocook is AND can pronounce it.

You can visit Berlin, New London, Bethlehem, Lisbon, Lebanon, and Dublin all in one afternoon.

Your snow blower gets stuck on the roof.

Your barn is bigger than your house.

BIBLIOGRAPHY

Andrews, Steven. "Pumpkin Regatta Promises New Treats and Old Favorites" NH.com (October 3, 2007).

Blackman, W. Haden. *The Field Guide to North American Hauntings: Everything You Need to Know About Encountering Over 100 Ghosts, Phantoms, and Spectral Entities*. New York, New York: Three Rivers Press, 1998.

Citro, Joseph. *Curious New England: The Unconventional Travelers Guide to Eccentric Destinations*. Lebanon, New Hampshire: University Press of New England, 2004.

Clayton, John. *You Know You're in New Hampshire When . . .*Guilford, Connecticut: The Globe Pequot Press, 2005.

"Commodore Nutt: The History of the Well Known Dwarf". *The New York Times* (May 26, 1881).

D'Agostino, Thomas. "Haunted New Hampshire". Atglen, Pennsylvania: Schiffer Books, 2007.

Davis, Jeremy K. *Lost Ski Areas of the White Mountains*. Charleston, South Carolina: The History Press, 2008.

D'Entremont, Jeremy. "Boon Island Light" Lighthouse.cc.

Drake, Samuel. "New England Legends and Folk Lore" Secaucus NJ: Castle Books, 1993.

Feals, Jennifer. 'Exposure: Jeremy D'Entremont, Lighthouse Enthusiast" Seacoastonline.com.

Filgate, Michelle. "Portsmouth Ghost Stories" Main Street Magazine.

Gore, Moody P. and Speare, Guy E. "New Hampshire Folk Tales". 1932, Plymouth, New Hampshire.

Gosling, Nick. "Ghosts, Murderers, and Beer" WireNH.com, October 26, 2005.

Goudsward, David and Stone, Robert E. *America's Stonehenge: The Mystery Hill Story.* Wellesley, Massachusetts: Branden Books, 2003.

Jameson, W.C. *Buried Treasure of New England: Legends of Hidden Riches, Forgotten War Loots, and Lost Ship Treasures.* Atlanta, Georgia: August House Publishers, 1998.

Johnson, Chloe. "UFOs: Is Seeing Believing? A Retired UNH Professor Says the Truth is Out There" The Citizen of Laconia. February 24, 2008.

Johnson, Scott A. "The Isles of Shoals" HorrorChannel.com.

Jones, Eric. "New England Curiosities: Quirky Characters, Roadside Oddities and Other Offbeat Stuff " Globe Pequot Press. 2006, Guilford, Connecticut.

Jordan, Charles J. *Tales Told in the Shadows of the White Mountains.* Lebanon, New Hampshire: University Press of New England, 2003.

Manning, Erin. "Whispers, Rumors, Legends, and Stuff We Heard". *HippoPress* (October 25, 2001).

McDonald, Joyce. "In the Shelter of Monadnock: Jaffrey, New Hampshire, Cather's Favorite Retreat and Final Resting Place." The Willa Cather Archive (www.cather.unl.edu) July 2009.

O'Connor, Marianne. *Haunted Hikes of New Hampshire.*

Parker, Gail Underwood. *More than Petticoats: Remarkable New Hampshire Women.* Guilford, CT: Morris Book Publishers, 2009.

Pinder, Eric. *Among the Clouds: Work, Wit & Wild Weather at the Mount Washington Observatory.* Alpine Books, 2008.

Pinder, Eric. *Tying Down the Wind: Adventures in the Worst Weather on Earth.* New York, New York: Penguin Group, 2000.

Robinson, J. Dennis "As I Please: The Truth about Ocean Born Mary" SeacoastNH.com.

Rogak, Lisa. "Stones and Bones of New England: A Guide to unusual, Historic, and otherwise Notable Cemeteries" The Globe Pequot Press. 2004, Guildford, Connecticut.

Rogers, Barbara Radcliff and Stillman. *New Hampshire Off the Beaten Path.* Guilford, Connecticut: GPP Travel Books, 2007.

Rule, Rebecca. *Live Free and Eat Pie.* Frenchboro, Maine: Islandport Press, 2008.

Saxon, Arthur H. *P.T. Barnum: The Legend and the Man.* New York, New York: The Columbia University Press, 1995.

Thorpe, L.Ashton. *Manchester of Yesterday.* Manchester, New Hampshire: Granite State Press, 1939.

INTERNET RESOURCES

The following websites were essential in the research of *Strange New Hampshire*:

BigfootEncounters.com
BloodCemetery.com
CowHampshire.com
Cryptozoology.com
GoNewEngland.com
GraveMatter.com
HollowHill.com
ManchesterNH.gov
NewEnglandCuriosities.com
NewEnglandGhosts.com
NewHampshire.com
NHGraveyards.org
NHHistory.org
NH.Searchroots.com
NHTourGuide.com
PoliticalGraveyard.com
StrangeNE.com
Valley-Cemetary.com
Wikipedia.org

INDEX